IIII I IIIIIIIII IIII IIII III
I0065431

Right Questions at the Right Time

Smart Systemic Questions.

Positive Psychology, Effective
Communication, and Transformational
Leadership Techniques

for Leaders, Consultants, and Coaches

Logan Mind

Copyright © 2024 - All rights reserved.

No part of this book may be reproduced in any form or by any electronic or mechanical means, including information storage and retrieval systems, without written permission from the author, except for the use of brief quotations in a book review.

EXTRAS

logan.decodemymind.com/allbooks

Workbooks

Meditations

Affirmations

Audiobooks

DOWNLOAD

@loganmindpsychology

How to Download Your Extras

One of the most valuable aspects of this book extends beyond the final page. It encompasses a range of practical, easily accessible extras that are key to ensuring the application of the book's insights to your personal growth and professional development. Among these is the downloadable PDF 21-Day Challenge, an audiobook version (when available), a free complementary book on 'Emotional Intelligence,' a curated link to all my other works, and an opportunity for you to provide honest feedback via a designated link.

Downloading the PDF 21-Day Challenge is a critical step in internalizing the principles detailed in the book. Why? Because knowledge, while invaluable, only becomes transformative through consistent practice. The challenge is designed to guide you day-by-day, encouraging the application of systemic questions, positive psychology, effective communication, and transformational leadership techniques in your daily interactions and decision-making processes.

Moreover, the complementary audiobook ensures that the profound insights of the book are accessible regardless of your preferred learning style or busy schedule. Whether you're commuting, exercising, or simply relaxing, the audiobook aims to seamlessly integrate personal growth into your daily routine.

The inclusion of a free book on 'Emotional Intelligence' serves to further deepen your understanding of effective communication and leadership. Emotional intelligence is the cornerstone of building resilient, supportive, and collaborative relationships both in your personal and professional life. Offering this book underlines the commitment to providing comprehensive tools for your development.

Accessible via a special link, you'll also find a wealth of my other books related to improving personal and professional competencies.

Each book is geared towards nurturing skills and insights that complement the transformational journey you've started with this book.

The Importance of Your Feedback

Your honest feedback is invaluable, especially for an independent author like myself. It doesn't take much time to share your thoughts, yet this small action has a profound impact. Constructive feedback not only assists me in refining and improving my work but also in supporting and guiding future readers in their decision-making process. Just think, a few minutes of your time could dramatically shape the concept's impact on others. Your insights, experiences, and suggestions are immensely appreciated and taken to heart.

To access these invaluable resources, simply click on the link or scan the QR code provided. Once on the landing page, click on the book cover you've purchased, and you'll be able to download all the related extras directly.

Your endeavor into tapping into the power of asking the right questions at the right time is further enhanced with these extras. The designed practicality woven into both the book and the extras aims at facilitating a metamorphosis that accentuates your abilities to communicate effectively, lead with vigor, and build sustaining relationships. This arsenal of resources doesn't just accompany your reading journey; it transforms it into a hands-on approach to self-improvement and leadership.

Claiming Your Extras

To claim your extras, simply click or scan the QR code in the image provided. A page will display where selecting the cover of the book you purchased proceeds to unlock all the mentioned extras for download.

Check out the extras here:

[https://logan.decodemymind.com/allbooks]

Taking advantage of these extras not only deepens your comprehension but also ensures the implementable takeaways are woven into the fabric of your daily life. The path to applying systemic questions, imbibing positive psychology, mastering effective communication, and embodying transformational leadership is here. Make the most of this opportunity to enhance both your intrapersonal and interpersonal skills, setting a strong foundation for continued personal and professional success.

Chapter 1: The Power of Asking the Right Systemic Questions.

Knowing the right questions to ask... I mean, it sounds simple enough, right? But here's where things get juicy. It's not just about shooting off a question, it's about asking the right ones - the kind that opens a can of worms (in a good way, mind you), peeling back layers to get to the crux of what we want to know or, more importantly, what we need to know.

Have you ever had a moment where one question, a seemingly innocuous one, changed everything for you? Like, it flipped a switch in your brain? I have, and trust me, it's as dramatic as it sounds. It made me realize the power that lies in the art of asking. Not in a nosy-parker kind of way, but in a strategic, unlocking doors you didn't even know were there kind of way.

This chapter is about just that: systemic questions that do more than just scratch the surface. Think of it as your behind-the-scenes pass. Those questions that make you go, "Hmm, I never thought about it like that," because, let's be honest, who doesn't love those little lightbulb moments? They're what move us from where we are to, well, somewhere better, more informed - whether we're talking about work, personal growth, or even relationships.

But, I'm not just here to chat about asking questions as if it were as easy as asking your smart speaker the weather. No, no. It's an art full of nuances, personal reflections, and yes, even a bit of psychology. There's a tact to doing this in a way that not only makes sense but feels natural, too. And getting it right? Well, that's where the magic lies. So, stick around for some candid stories, personal reflections, and, dare I say, game-changing insights.

Understanding Systemic Questions and Their Importance

So, what's the big deal with systemic questions, and why should you even care? Well, let me tell you, if you're looking to get a grip on the complexities of team or family dynamics, **systemic questions** are your golden ticket. It's like switching from looking at a still photo to watching a dynamic movie scene. You get to see all the action, not just a snapshot.

First off, we've got to grasp the difference between **linear** and **systemic questions**. Linear questions are the straightforward ones—like asking "Who did what?" They don't really dig deeper into the context or relationships at play. On the other hand, systemic questions are the brain-teasers. They make you think about the relationships, patterns, and structures within a complex system, like a company or family.

I remember this one time, I was working with a team, and there was this cycle of **miscommunication** and **frustration** brewing under the surface. It was when I started asking systemic questions like, "How does John's way of communicating affect the way the team collaborates?" that we began to see the bigger picture. It's incredible how these questions can unravel the fabric of how people interact within a system, allowing them to reflect on their actions and see how everything's connected.

"Systemic questioning is like a mirror, reflecting not just your face, but the whole room behind you."

One gem in the chest of systemic questioning techniques is **circular questioning**. It's all about asking questions in a way that reflects back on the asker and other parties involved, promoting deep reflection. Consider asking, "How do you think your sister feels when arguments break out during family dinners?" Suddenly, everyone starts **thinking**, not just about their feelings but how their actions generate ripples within the family.

"In asking, we are also seeking to understand our role in the cosmic dance of interactions."

Using these questions doesn't just help in **family therapy sessions**; they're legit game changers in team settings too. It nudges members towards understanding how their behaviors, agreements, and disagreements impact the collective mission. Imagine kick-starting a meeting with, "How can we each contribute to a more efficient workflow, considering our recent hurdles?" Suddenly, the focus shifts from individual tasks to collective outcomes.

So, why are systemic questions so powerful? They couch **effective communication, complex connection exploration, and the stimulating of understanding** within an inquiry. In essence, they prompt us to think in networks, understanding the interdependence of our actions in the webs we are part of. Implement these questions and watch as they transform **miscommunication and conflict into cohesion and insight**—essential tools for anyone in coaching, leadership, or consultancy roles.

Finally, let me leave you with a small **exercise**. Next time you're faced with a dilemma within your team or family, try framing your thoughts into a systemic question. Look beyond the surface issue and consider the dynamic interplay of relationships and past events leading up to this moment. Not only will this help in stimulating a collective understanding, but it could also open doors to unexpected solutions. Trust me, the insight you gain might just turn those prevailing issues into ancient history.

The Role of Positive Psychology in Forming Questions

Isn't it curious how a simple question can stir up opinions, emotions, or even lead to a groundbreaking idea? I have always marveled at the power of the **right** question... and when you pair this with the principles of positive psychology, you've got something even more special.

Positive psychology principles aren't just there to put a smile on our faces—though they do a pretty fine job of that, too. But rather, they're mostly about steering us toward a deeper understanding of our resilience and capacity for growth. Now, thinking about applying these principles alongside systemic questioning techniques practically screams opportunity for coaches and leaders to ignite significant developments within their teams and, why not admit, themselves.

So, let me take a tad more direct approach by saying, the gist is fairly straight-forward: construct inquiries through a lens of positivity. For example, rather than asking "Why does our team always falter?" try, "What strengths can we leverage to improve our teamwork?" Imagine the difference this shift in perspective can bring to an inquisitive exploration of team dynamics.

("Transform setbacks into setups for future successes...")

Systemic questions, well they've got a charm that when tossed into the mix with some emotional well-being spice, you all meet on this nice playground infused with self-awareness and empathy. We're talking families sticking closer, teams achieving their targets because members not merely acknowledge, but value others' viewpoint, creatively overcoming challenges.

Incorporating Gratitude, Forgiveness, and Mindfulness

I've noticed, nothing sets a tone like gratitude. It sounds... whimsical, right? But it's science, trust me! Sprinkle in forgiveness, you're on a roll to mend or strengthen relations, irking away gnarly knots of resentment. And mindfulness? Think of this as your brain taking a chill pill, tuning in like never before.

Let's Briefly Tackle Circular Questioning

Fun fact here: This technique asks questions that not only allows but **encourages** multiple perspectives. Like, "How do each of you, see others contributing to the strength of this unit?" Now, weave in positivity enveloped queries:

1. **Start with gratitude-based questions**: "What are we truly thankful for in this team/family?"
2. **Slide towards forgiveness**: "How might letting go of any grudges supercharge our collaboration?"
3. **Promote mindfulness**: "In what moments do we find ourselves completely engaged and absorbed?"

Here's something to ponder...

("A question doesn't merely voice a curiosity, it's an invisible thread binding individuals in shared insights...")

By encouraging these types of reflections, aren't we indirectly coaching individuals towards nurturing growth, recognizing strengths, and building positive relationships among teammates and family members? Think about it—the question isn't a catalyst but a vessel transporting us from point A, 'the unknown', to B, 'understanding and transformation'.

And to really bring this home with a practical touch: Try this at your next meeting or family dinner—start with a positive, systemic question. Track how the dynamics shift, how the room's energy changes. No grand gestures, just genuine curiosity wrapped in goodwill. If stimulating a thriving environment with happy, highly effective teams and families was a puzzle, consider positive, systemic questions a crucial piece.

How Effective Communication is Achieved Through Inquiry

Ah, the art of communication—a real game-changer, right? Or at least, it should be. Let's consider a curious method that seems to cut through the clutter like a hot knife through butter: **systemic questioning.** Trust me, it's more interesting than it sounds.

Now, imagine sitting in a meeting, or maybe at a family dinner—tensions high, everyone ready to toss in their two cents. Instead of the usual chaos, someone starts **asking open-ended, non-judgmental questions.** Suddenly, the room shifts. People lean in, ears perked, ready to share. That's because they feel heard, understood, maybe even a little bit valued.

*"An empty vessel makes the most noise, but ask the **right question,** and it might just fill with gold."*

Developing **effective communication strategies** begins and ends with the right kind of questioning. **Systemic questioning techniques** aren't just clever ways to get information. They're keys to unlocking partnerships, understanding, and yep, those all-important problem-solving scenarios.

Ever been part of a team where every meeting feels like rowing upstream? By virtue of posing thoughtfully shaped **questions**, you essentially extend an olive branch to the others involved. These questions build the foundation of **rapport and trust** in literary seconds. A question shows you care—or, at least, that you're willing to.

Consider this mantra:

"Open-ended questions are open doors to a person's thought palace—walk in with respect."

Questions such as "*What do you think led us to this outcome?*", or "*How do your experiences shape your view on this?*" don't just sound good; they peel back layers, revealing the core of an issue or stance. It moves us from accusatory glances to understanding nods.

Switching gear to **circular questioning**—I hear you asking, "*What in the world is that?*" It's a technique where you explore the relationships between people and their narratives by rotating questions among them. This isn't just for the folks in family therapy seeking understanding but also for teams looking to understand their dynamics better.

- Let's take Kevin, who's always at Angela's throat during meetings.
- Asking, "*Kevin, what do you think Angela means when she brings up X?*", engages Kevin to consider her perspective. Spicer still, ask Angela to reflect on what Kevin hears her say.

Swap out accusations with curiosity, and watch the magic unfold. By inviting each to reflect on these perceptions openly, **collaboration blossoms**. It's inviting **active listening** into the room—a sure sign communication is on the uptick.

Bringing systemic questions into **conflict resolutions** is akin to being a conductor of a chaotic orchestra—within chaos, there's rhythm, patterns, and solutions, all exposed through diligent inquiry. "*What outcome would be meaningful for all of us?*" Such questions beckon collaboration like bees to honey.

In urls of team meetings or talk therapy requisite settings where emotions are often high, and perspectives clash, hitting the pause button and shifting gears to systemic enquiry can change the course of action, **build bridges, and importantly, foster solutions where stalemates once loomed.**

Starting small, let's *exercise usin contextual enquiry next time we find ourselves at a junction.* Posing a question about how team

14

members feel a project is going, or how family members see a solution to an ongoing disagreement can start laying the cobblestones for a path forward. These approaches, loaded with the **powers of enquiry,** don't merely clear the fog; they paint the sky with possibility.

Whether a coach, leader, or developer is listening and learning, tapping into the well of systemic inquiry reshapes our engagements into experiences marked with understanding, collaboration, and yes—effective communication. Let's not just converse but connect, not just speak but resonate, with each dawn, asking... the **right question** at the **right** time.

Introduction to Transformational Leadership Through Questions

When was the last time someone asked you a question that really made you think? Not just any question, but one that stirred something inside of you, compelling you to consider a perspective you've never entertained before. That's the power of asking the right **systemic questions,** something indispensable in the realm of transformational leadership.

So, let's get to the heart of the matter: **Why do certain questions have the power to initiate positive change within teams or families?** Well, it boils down to the essence of **transformative leadership**. This brand of leadership is all about encouraging growth and positive change, *not just* in terms of targets and achievements, but also in attitudes, approaches, and mindsets. This kind of change requires a deep understanding of the complex dynamics at play, a task that might seem daunting at first.

The thing is, the complexity doesn't have to leave us feeling overwhelmed. **Systemic questioning** lightens the load, **significantly**. It crafts a **collaborative, empowering** environment that actively involves each team or family member in the problem-solving process. Imagine planting a seed and watching it grow, but in this case, the seed is your question, and the growth? Well, that's the collective brainstorming, soul-searching, and breakthroughs that follow.

Let me paint you a picture: consider **circular questions**. These aren't your run-of-the-mill queries; they're crafted to promote reflection and insight among individuals and groups. For instance, **"How do you think your reaction might affect the attitude of the rest of the team?"** This type of question encourages self-reflection and awareness of one's impact on the larger group dynamic, highlighting the interconnectedness of individual actions and collective outcomes.

"A question not only seeks an answer but invites deeper thought and shared explorations toward possible futures."

Embedding **systemic questioning techniques** in your toolbox as a transformational leader guides your team towards desired outcomes with a sense of shared purpose. These techniques may include asking open-ended questions that stimulate discussion, using hypotheticals to explore possible scenarios, and employing reflective questions that encourage individuals to consider their role within the team or family system.

By harnessing these techniques, you, as a leader or consultant, tackle challenges with a more nuanced, holistic approach. These aren't Band-Aid fixes; they're steps towards lasting, positive transformation. Here's how you could integrate systemic questioning into your leadership style:

- **Create a 'question-friendly' environment**: Make it clear that every question is welcome, that every dissent or curiosity builds the team rather than break it down.
- **Practice, practice, practice**: The more you integrate systemic questions into your daily interactions, the more intuitive they will become.

- **Reflect on the effectiveness of your questions**: Not every question will hit the mark, and that's OK. Reflecting on what worked and what didn't is part of honing your skill.

"Empowerment emerges when individuals perceive their role as pivotal within the collective pathway towards success."

Taking this a step further, let's discuss some **real-life stories and examples**. Remember the team leader who managed to turn around his department's flagging morale? His secret weapon was systemic questioning. By asking his team members thoughtful, open-ended questions about their perceptions and ideas for improvement, he engaged them as active participants in co-creating their success story.

Utilizing systemic questioning isn't just a leadership strategy, it's a commitment to unlocking the collective intelligence and creativity of your team or family, stimulating an environment where growth and positive transformation are not just possible but inevitable. It's about pushing boundaries, exploring possibilities, and, most importantly, believing in the power of the right questions at the right time.

The Impact of Timing in Posing Systemic Questions

Let's dive right in by acknowledging how crucial the timing is when we talk about asking the right questions, especially in contexts like team meetings and family therapy sessions. There's something like a rhythm, you know? A kind of dance between when you speak and when you listen. This not only helps in making sure that your message lands but also that it does so in a way that stimulates constructive and meaningful dialogue.

So, let's tackle the idea of **systemic questions** and why the "when" is as important as the "what." Systemic questions aren't just any questions. They're designed to probe deeper into the underlying structures of a team or a family's dynamics. They make you think, rethink and come to those lightbulb moments. And yet, it's not just what you ask... but, you've guessed it, when you ask.

- **Recognizing significance:** I cannot stress this enough. There are moments that are just ripe for certain types of questions. During a team debrief after a project, for instance, it might be prime time to ask reflective questions that explore lessons learned.

"Questions have power - a lot of it. But their true power unleashes by timing. Wait for the moment, or create it, but never rush it."

Let's talk types. There are several types of systemic questions – lineal, circular, strategic, reflexive. Each has its place, but here's the tricky part: Identifying this place.

- **Lineal questions** work wonders when you're dealing with concrete problems. Let's say you need to pinpoint a process hitch during your meeting. You're looking at the cause and effect here—straight, direct.
- **Circular questions**, though? They're about perspectives. Picture this: "How do you think your workload affects the team's overall deadline?" It suddenly opens up a vista of viewpoints.
- **Strategic questions** are a bit more aimed. You're trying to guide someone towards a realization or decision but subtly.
- **Reflexive questions** reflect back on the person. They encourage introspection. "How did your approach to the project impact your personal growth?"

Now, applying skilled judgment to determine when exactly to pose these questions... well, that can feel like an art form. And it kind of is. It's about reading the room, understanding the current atmosphere, emotions, and the conversation's flow. It requires practice, mistakes, yes, and then learning from those mistakes.

Understanding the **influence of timing** on communication dynamics is a considerable part of this. Communicate too early, and you're not heeding the room's energy; too late, and the moment has passed, rendering the question ineffective or even irrelevant...

Developing an awareness? Look, it's about more than just paying attention. It requires, dare I say, a fascination with human behavior, interactions, and an earnest desire to facilitate progress.

"The perfect question at the perfect time can shift the entire group's direction. It's that pivotal."

Consider this your toolbox for timing:

- Observe before you interact. The mood, the context, the subtle dynamics.
- Reflect on your objective with each question. Are you trying to clarify, understand, motivate, or challenge?
- Practice! Sorry, no way around this. Experience sharpens your ability to gauge timing like nothing else.

In essence, mastering the timing of systemic questions turns a mere conversation into a journey of discovery. Importantly, it's about creating spaces where people feel seen and heard, where dialogue can flow in a direction that fosters understanding, opens up new vistas of thinking, and, most crucially, guides your team or family unit across the bridges of comprehension and cooperation.

So, to all coaches, leaders, consultants out there— remember, asking the right question is good, but asking it at just the right moment? Now, that's where the magic happens.

Building a Foundation for Advanced Inquiry Techniques

In a world brimming with questions, what **truly matters** is not just how we ask but what we ask. It's like sorting through a maze – some routes lead to dead ends; others pave the way to the treasure. In building a foundation for advanced inquiry techniques, understanding the **art of asking the right systemic questions** is pivotal to unlocking mysteries within complex systems, be it in coaching, leadership, or consulting. Think of it as **sherlocking** through the convoluted twists and turns of organizational dilemmas.

Firstly, mastery in systemic questioning does not sprout overnight. It's layered, demands patience, and a bit of what I like to call a 'curiosity fest'. **Curiosity**, that unquenchable thirst for understanding, lies at the heart of systemic inquiry. And, like building any good habit, it starts with practice, coupled with a generous dash of courage – to ask, to probe, and to question the status quo.

Imagine walking into a room where a team is grappling with low morale and declining performance. The impulse? Provide solutions, wave the magic wand that doesn't really exist. However, if equipped with systemic questioning techniques, you approach differently.

"What patterns are emerging here that we haven't noticed?"

"Who holds the information that could reshape our understanding of this problem?"

These kinds of questions steer us away from fruitless ventures and surface-level fixes, enabling us to dig deeper into the fabric of the problem. It's like taking a timeout to question if what we're seeing on the surface is merely an illusion. Only then can we start eine collage of potential pioneers; those invisible threads waiting to be pulled that bring unraveling layers of understanding.

Take Jenny, for example, a mid-level manager who felt like she was always two steps behind. It wasn't until she pivoted to **asking systemic questions** focused on patterns, boundaries, and structures that she began to see the bigger picture—a revelation that how her team interacted internally echoed external inefficiencies.

"Every question we ask is a door to a new path, a path yet unseen and unknown, waiting to be explored."

By cultivating (and it does require a bit of a green thumb, metaphorically speaking) a practice of regular inquiry, checking our biases, and entertaining multiple perspectives... well, we compound our ability to explore complexities with enhanced clarity.

Consider an exercise borrowed from the art of reflective journaling. Spend a week documenting the questions you ask in your professional environment. Categorize them:

- Are they **operational**, aiming to resolve day-to-day hiccups?
- Or are they **strategic and systemic**, aiming to unravel deeper undercurrents?

"The questions we shy away from asking are often the keys to unlocking entrenched barriers."

Day by day, this simple reflection triggers a shift; patterns start to emerge, revealing the kinds of questions that lead to impactful insights — indicating where your question-asking muscle needs a workout.

So, stepping into the terrain of systemic questions is akin to preparing for a rigorous expedition. It's essential to equip oneself with gusto, resilience, and an intrinsic **motivation to probe** beneath the surface. Armed with the power of **effective questioning**, leaders, coaches, and consultants can transform the landscapes of their fields, stimulating environments where curiosity breeds innovation and solutions are merely the right questions away.

Now, let's put these questioning caps on, and may your inquiries pave the path to findings most profound and transformative. And just maybe, when pondering the next complex dilemma, **the right questions** will illuminate the darkest corners, showing that perhaps, the answers were in front of us all along, cloaked merely in our ability to ask.

Practical Exercise

Alright, let's roll up our sleeves and dive—figuratively speaking!—into a hands-on exercise that focuses on Chapter 1: The Power of Asking the Right Systemic Questions. If you're a coach, leader, or consultant out there in the wild, complex world of organizational dynamics, this one's crafted with you in mind. We're going to tackle this with a bit of chit-chat style, forget the stiff upper lip and all that jazz.

Step 1: Pick Your Poison...Uh, Situation

First things first, think of a predicament or a challenge you're currently facing in your work environment. It could range from team dynamics gone awry, a project that's swerving off the planned path, or maybe you're struggling to inspire your team towards a shared vision. You know, the kind of stuff that makes you want to pull your hair out?

Step 2: Questioning Galore

Here comes the fun part...questions! Grab a pen and jot down every question that comes to your mind about your chosen situation. Yes, I mean everything, even if it sounds silly or you think it's irrelevant. Why? Because sometimes, those off-the-cuff questions can lead to breakthroughs. We're full detectives now, looking for clues everywhere.

Step 3: Playing Favorites

Got a solid list? Awesome! Now, highlight the **five questions** that you think could really get to the heart of the matter. These should be the kind of questions that, if answered, could provide genuine insights or open up new pathways for solutions. Think about questions that tackle the problem from a systemic angle — we're talking big, airy, broad daylight kind of questions that could lead to those "Aha!" moments.

Step 4: Interview Time

Here's the twist – find a colleague or friend, preferably someone who understands your work context but isn't too involved in the problem you've picked. Set up a mock interview where they play the role of an external consultant, asking you your selected systemic questions. The catch? Answer as transparently and thoughtfully as possible. This step is gold — believe me.

Personal reflection aside, you'd be surprised at how talking things out with someone slightly removed from the issue can offer new perspectives. It's like, they're not wearing the same glasses as we are, so they see things differently. Wild, right?

Step 5: Reflect and Plan

After the interview, spend some time reflecting on the insights gained. Were there any surprises? Lightbulb moments? Take notes on these insights and start formulating a rough plan on how to tackle the issue at hand. Think of this as sculpting – but instead of clay, you're using your newfound insights and perspectives.

And voilà! There you go, a practical, hands-on exercise derived from the power of asking the right systemic questions. Perfect for coaches, leaders, and consultants tirelessly working to make sense of the complexities within their organizations.

So, give this a whirl and see where it leads. Remember, the gold is often hidden under piles of 'regular' – it's up to us to dig it out. And hey, have a bit of fun with it! After all, every bit of wisdom gained here is another step towards becoming a maestro in handling organizational dynamics. Go knock it out of the park!

Chapter 2: Decoding the Elements of Effective Systemic Questions

So, you've dipped your toes in Chapter 1, getting a brief lay of the land, and now, we're about to wade a little deeper into the waters of systemic questioning. What's that, you ask? Well, it's quite the journey—figuring out how to ask the right questions, and I'm here to guide you through it, step by step.

Now, let me tell you... mastering the art of systemic questions isn't just about throwing together fancy, complex words in hope they stick and make sense. Nope, it's way more personal and meaningful. It's about connecting on a deeper level, you know? There's this uncanny power embedded in asking the right question at the right time—like unlocking a door you didn't even notice was there before (yes, I'm being serious).

I've been there before, scratching my head, wondering what went wrong in a conversation. Turns out, I was missing the mark with my questions—either too broad, too narrow, or just plain off-topic. And honestly, figuring this stuff out took some trial and... well, let's call it "a learning process."

In this chapter, we're gonna chat (yes, just like old friends) about how to craft questions that hit the nail on the head. You know, the kind that fosters genuine communication and brings out those hidden gems in everyday dialogues. And yes, there will be examples— because who doesn't love a good story to illustrate a point?

It's kinda like being a detective, but instead of solving mysteries (though that could be fun), you're peeling back layers, getting to the juicy center of conversations. It sounds challenging, might even cause some head-scratching moments, but stick with me.

Through personal gaffes, (uh, a ton of those) and moments of "Aha!", I've gathered some insights that might just shed some light on how asking smarter, not harder, could be your best move yet.

Ready to explore the nitty-gritty? Great, because understanding the elements of effective systemic questions could pleasantly surprise you, changing how you engage in conversations forever. And who knows, by the end, we might all be a little closer to becoming the master conversationalists we secretly wish to be.

The Anatomy of a Powerful Question

In the world of meaningful conversations and impactful leadership, understanding how, or maybe more importantly, understanding the **why** behind the crafting of powerful, systemic questions really does come down to a few foundational ingredients.

First things first, let's chat about **starting with clear intentions.** Yeah, I know, it sounds simple. But trust me, identifying the specific outcome you're looking for when tossing a question into the ring is - and I can't stress this enough - paramount. It's like starting a journey, but you've actually got a map so you're not just wandering around hoping to stumble upon hidden treasure.

And while we're on this journey, let's consider how we're framing our questions.

Here's a little something to chew on:

"Words, so simple yet so powerful, choose ones that open doors."

Going with words like 'what' and avoiding the often accusatory loaded 'why' can really change the game. It's about **framing with compassion and curiosity.** The goal? Pull down those defensive walls and build bridges of understanding. Super corny? Absolutely. But true? Definitely.

Next up, we've got **open-endedness**. This isn't just an, "Oh, nice to add on if we remember," kind of thing. No, this is the bread and butter of engagement. You're looking for more than a "yes" or "no." Encourage, no – **inspire** glimpses into thoughts, feelings, experiences.

And allow me to introduce you to – the heart, the soul - the five "A"s of crafting these types of questions:

- **Affirming:** Make them feel seen.
- **Autonomy-supportive:** Give them the wheel.
- **Actionable:** Spark ideas for steps forward.
- **Audience-specific:** Tailor-make your question sweater.
- **Asking about something clear but unknown:** It's not mysterious for the sake of being edgy. It's inviting exploration.

Now, why does any of this matter? You might ponder as you - hopefully - lean in, intrigued. Simply put,

"The questions we ask direct the stories we tell."

Consider this, a question can be a window into not just the mind but also the heart. Imagine you have the opportunity to not only hear responses but to listen to dreams, fears, the very essence of a person. That's the gold we're here for.

Alright, let's dial this down to you – yes, *you* reading this. Think about the last major conversation you had. Could be at work with a team, or home with a partner or a friend. What was the flavor of your questions? Did you sprinkle them with **compassion** and **curiosity.** Were they open enough to invite a story rather than a yes or no? And, did they align with our **dashing five "A"s.**

You see, once you get the hang of this, it becomes a sort of second nature. Ingredients in your communication kitchen you reach for without a second thought – transforming not just the questions you ask, but the richness of the conversations you have.

I invite you, then, as you go comma about your day, to consciously perform a little experiment. Infuse your conversations with these tempered tips. It might feel like you're not doing anything *dramatically* different at first. But, give it time. Powerful, systemic questions have a way of quietly revolutionizing the conversations you're a part of – making them brighter, deeper, and infinitely more meaningful.

So go on, lead with intention, frame with kindness, dare to ask openly, and don't forget the five "A"s. You might just be surprised at the stories that unfold.

Distinguishing Between Open and Closed Questions

When attempting to foster meaningful conversations, the shift between asking open and closed questions can either make or break the dialogue. Let's explore the arsenal of strategic communication. The crux of effective dialogue lies in **identifying the desired outcomes for each question type**. We're talking harvesting the broad, reflective panoramas with open questions, versus the sharp, succinct precision of closed questions for immediate clarity. See the beauty? Open questions are all about stimulating exploration. They're like opening a door... wondering what's on the other side. Closed questions, on the other hand, are about validating understanding, making sure we're all on the same page.

But, how do we **strategically balance both types**? The answer is simpler than one might think. Weave open questions to sketch the big picture, exploring issues in their full glory. Then hone in with closed questions for that all-important clarification. It's almost like scaffolding your conversation to build it higher and stronger.

Consider this:

"The ability to ask the right question is more than half the battle of finding the answer."

Now think about **how people respond differently** to these question types. Open questions prompt reflection, introspection, and often, a cascade of further discussion. They light up the path for new ideas and perspectives to blossom. Closed questions, conversely, equip us for immediate decision-making – a requisite in moments demanding swift responses.

Understanding this dance is key. But here's where it gets more nuanced. We've got to **assess question context**. It's like choosing, say, the right type of glasses for reading versus sunglasses for the beach. Closed questions rock in formal evaluations and surveys—clean, efficient, and to the point. Open questions, though? They truly shine in coaching sessions or personal discovery endeavors, where the journey itself uncovers gold. A line that sticks with me is this:

"Words are containers. They either contain freedom or they contain barriers."

(I found myself nodding at that, didn't you?) This thinking applies both to our professional and personal lives. Imagine integrating this into leadership tactics, performance reviews, or unity family dinners—powerful, right?

Here's your takeaway exercise (Feel free to actually try this out):

- Start your next conversation with an open question. Notice the difference?
- Follow up with a closed question to wrap your understanding.
- Reflect on the natural flow between the two and how it steers conversations.

Words start becoming less about 'talking' and more about 'connecting'... **The power of choosing wisely** cannot be understated. And really, that's what it's all about—adopting a strategy that enriches communication and relationships. Next time you find yourself at a crossroads in a conversation, remembering the right ingredient can turn an ordinary chat into a veritable feast of insights and understandings. So, when in doubt, toggle between the openness to explore and the closure to affirm. Become the maestro of your interactions, leading with finesse and purpose. Don't just speak. Speak effectively.

The Significance of Tone and Body Language

Ever wondered why some conversations just flow naturally and leave you feeling good, while others feel like trudging through mud, even when the words being said aren't all that different? It's not just about **what** you say, but **how** you say it, combining both your tone and your body language, which can either open doors to meaningful dialogue or slam them shut.

First off, keeping your tone **positive and confident** is a no-brainer, at least it seems so. But it's incredible, really, how a slight edge of hesitation in your voice... or a hint of doubt, can set off a chain reaction that closes the communication lines faster than a blink. So, make it a habit to voice your thoughts clearly, brightly – even if you're not feeling top of the world. It's catchy, believe me. People are more likely to engage in an open dialogue when the atmosphere feels lighter, more buoyant.

Now, let's get physical – I mean, let's talk body language. Maintaining eye contact comes up a lot, and yeah, it's important. But it's not about staring someone down. It's about showing that you're here, with them, genuinely interested in what they have to share. It's telling, the difference it makes, signaling that you're **paying attention**, which in today's world of endless distractions, is quite the compliment.

Speaking of paying attention, how often do we really notice the nonverbal cues others throw our way? People might not always say when they're uncomfortable, but their body screams it – closed postures, fidgeting, looking away. It's our job to catch these signals and respond accordingly. Maybe take a step back, switch topics gently, or simply acknowledging, "I get the feeling this isn't something you're comfortable diving into," can drastically change the energy of the conversation.

Getting rid of distractions might seem straightforward, but it's crucial for stimulating positive interactions. This means putting away phones, maybe finding a quieter spot – focusing on making the verbal and visual communication as clear as a day without clouds.

"The most important thing in communication is hearing what isn't said."

Ever pondered that gem of a line? It brilliantly encapsulates the essence of understanding nonverbal cues. Another might go something like:

"Your actions speak so loudly, I can hardly hear what you're saying."

These block quotes remind us, in a roundabout way, how our body language and tone can either make our words hit home or fade into the background.

I like to toss in a practical tip or two: Try practicing your tone and observing your body language in front of a mirror. Sounds silly? Maybe, but it works wonders. Or, engage in pretend conversations with a friend where you purposely alter your nonverbal signals. Try being closed off, then open and welcoming – and observe how the "feel" of the conversation shifts.

So you see, understanding and harnessing the power of tone and body language isn't rocket science, but it does ask for a bit of mindfulness and effort. And trust me, once you get the hang of it, there's no going back. The way you connect with people changes, transforming your interactions into more meaningful encounters. So go ahead, give it a shot – apply these pointers, and watch your conversations take a turn for the better..

Strategies for Formulating Impactful Questions

Knowing how to ask the **right questions** can feel like trying to grab a cloud with your bare hands – you know it's important, but how do you even start? Here's how: by tailoring your technique to fit the scenario at hand... Just like choosing the right tool from a toolbox, the context **determines** the best model to employ.

First off, let's talk about using PICO principles in **medical settings**. Ever heard of this? It stands for Patient, Intervention, Comparison, and Outcome. Sounds straightforward, right? By breaking down your clinical questions into these chunks, you're more likely to hit the nail on the head with your patient assessments. Picture this – you're assessing a patient with a chronic condition, instead of going in circles, you pinpoint what you need: "What's the intervention here, and how does it compare to the usual treatment?" Voila, you've set a clear path for understanding and action.

Next up, the SAFE model – a go-to during **coaching sessions**. This gem stands for Situation, Attitude, Feelings, and Exploration. It's brilliant for sparking deep reflection, helping the person you're coaching explore through their thoughts and emotions about a situation.

"How I feel about this project might differ wildly from how you see it,... and discussing our attitudes and feelings can uncover a lot of hidden assumptions. The **exploration part? That's where the magic happens."**

The STAR framework shines during **performance reviews**. Think Situations, Tasks, Actions, Results. It guides us in discussing specific examples, steering away from generic feedback. It brings clarity, making both praises and areas for improvement crystal clear.

"Providing clear examples of tasks, detailing the actions taken, and reflecting on the results helps in creating a fact-based conversation... similar to storytelling, but with actionable insights."

Now, let's talk teamwork with the DIY model: Data, Insights, Yours. I cannot begin to tell you how much this **simplifies** collaboration. Sharing data lays a common ground—everyone knows what we're dealing with. Sharing insights invites others into your thought process... And "Yours"? That's when you open the stage for others to contribute, stimulating true partnership.

Ever tried these approaches? Here's a little exercise to try next time you're warming up for a meeting or a one-on-one:

- Choose a **model** relevant to your situation – PICO for clinical questions, SAFE for coaching, STAR for reviews, or DIY for team discussions.
- **Prepare** a couple of 'model-specific' questions ahead of time.
- Swirl them in with your usual questioning style... see how it changes the dynamic, brings out different responses, or even shifts the energy of the conversation.
- Reflect after—did it spark **new conversations**? Did it bring any surprising insights?

Let's consider these **principles** not as restrictions but as springboards – means to pry open the treasure chest of effective communication. Remember, these models are not just about **asking**; they're about listening to what's said (and what's **not** said) in response. That's where the true gold lies.

"Asking the right question at the right time is more of an art than a science. Practice, reflect, adjust, and repeat... That's how you polish the art."

In a nutshell, these strategies aren't just helpful; they're transformative when applied with thought and care. So why not give them a spin in your next interaction? Who knows which doors of understanding they might **unlock**.

Avoiding Common Pitfalls in Questioning

When engaging in dialogue, whether in a leadership role, coaching, or even day-to-day conversations, it's surprisingly easy to fall into some traps. These obstacles, I've discovered through a series of trials and errors (and let's be honest, some face-palm moments), not only derail the path of effective communication—they also hinder the infrastructure of trust and openness we tirelessly build. I'd like to shed some light on four common stumbling blocks: leading questions, bombarding with too many inquiries, giving in to vagueness, and overemphasis on personal stories.

Leading questions, let me tell you, are a true communication killer. I remember once asking, "Don't you think our strategy is exciting and innovative?" only to be met with nods. However, the nods lacked conviction. The feedback I sought never surfaced. Why? Leading questions carry within them a sneakily embedded answer. In doing so, we inadvertently nudge (albeit with good intentions) our interlocutors toward what we perceive to be the desired answer—effectively silencing their genuine reactions and thoughts. To communicate effectively, one must foster an environment where open, uninfluenced responses can flourish.

Now, onto the trap of **asking too many questions at once**. Picture this: you're bombarded with a slew of inquiries in one go. Overwhelming, right? It's akin to being asked to juggle; instead of focusing on catching one ball expertly, you're scrambling not to drop any. It dilutes the quality and depth of responses. To truly dig deep, focus on one question at a time; give it the breathing room it needs to fully come to life in the answer.

The baffling world of **vague questions** is another field riddled with hole traps. I've noticed that questions like "What do you think about that?" are met with confused stares more than insightful answers. Specificity is your friend. It guides the response, providing clarity— a clear runway for thoughts to land smoothly. It turns "What do you think about that?" into "What specific aspects of the new concept do you envision challenging to implement?"

Personal stories—oh, how mesmerizing it is to fall into the allure of our own experiences. I'm guilty of often starting with "That reminds me of a time...", drifting away into lengthy tales. But here's the thing: an overemphasis on our stories inadvertently shifts the limelight onto us, potentially overshadowing the main objective— unlocking others' perspectives and knowledge. Sure, personal stories can bridge gaps and underscore a point, but they should sprinkle the discussion, not drown it.

"Listen more than you speak." A golden, albeit ironic tip considering the context.

Let's practice avoiding these pitfalls through short exercises. Next time you frame a question, pause. Ask yourself—Is it leading? Is it singular and focused? Does it elaborate sufficiently to spur a targeted response? Is my personal story assisting, or is it an unsolicited guest appearance?

"Questions open the doors to dialogue, but the right question thrusts it wide open."

In essence, exploring the terrain of effective questioning requires awareness, adaptability, and a pinch of strategic thinking...not to mention, a good amount of practice and reflection. And remember, perfection in communication isn't the goal—it's the journey of continuous improvement, connections, and those 'aha!' moments that truly enrich it.

Mastering the Art of Follow-up Questions

Listening... learning to do it like you mean it, really getting into the nitty-gritty of what someone is saying, might just be the most underrated skill in the book when it comes to effective communication. Sure, we all "listen," but how often do we delve deep, knit our brows, and really, truly tune in? Less often than we think, I'm guessing.

First off, demonstrating **engagement and appreciation** isn't just a box to tick. It's about showing you're in this conversation for real. "I'm all ears," you might say. You lean in a bit. We've all been on the receiving end of half-baked listening—you can feel it, right? When someone's eyes glaze over as you're pouring your heart out. So, don't be that person.

Now, onto probing—gently, of course. Imagine your conversational partner has just shared something significant, but there's a layer you sense remains unexplored. "Can you tell me more about that?" is a gentle nudge without a push. It's about encouraging more depth, more insight, without making them feel like they're under the spotlight.

An insightful leader once said, "Every person you meet has something to teach you." That's struck with me. It's like saying, listen up because everyone has their unique knowledge to share. Who knows what you're about to uncover next?

Speaking of unfolding stories, acknowledging what's being shared isn't just polite—**it's key to building trust.** "I appreciate you sharing that," can work wonders. It's a simple way to validate their contribution. And hey, everyone likes to feel heard, understood, respected—like what they've got to say matters because, in reality, it does.

As for facilitating next steps, well, that's about figuring out where to from here. Seems obvious, but it's often missed. It's like when you finish a good yarn, and there's a moment of, "So, what happens now?" Outlining what comes next, and agreeing on clear expectations moves things forward. **It's teamwork in action.**

Once read a piece of advice, "Never leave a meeting without agreeing on the next action." It's simple but gold. Leaves nobody guessing what's to happen next, you know?

So, let's get real practical...

- Listening isn't just about hearing words. It's being attentive to the feeling, the unsaid. It's the pauses, the sighs, the unspoken truths lurking between lines.
- Asking follow-up questions - keep them open-ended, stimulating thought rather than a simple yes/no.
- Express genuine gratitude for shared insights. Seriously, a "thank you" can go miles.
- Be explicit about next steps to avoid that dreadful silence of, "what now?" A shared understanding of the forthcoming actions eliminates confusion and paves a straight path forwards.

Funny how these elements mirror much of life, don't you think? Success isn't just about the big wins or grand gestures; it's the tiny, thoughtful elements—notice how it's always those little things?—that make all the difference. Being a stellar communicator, asking the right follow-up questions... it's very much about tuning in to the details, pounding the pavement, and sometimes, letting instinct guide the way.

Remember when I mentioned engaging genuinely? Here's a quick exercise - next time you're in a conversation, every time you're tempted to interrupt or steal the stage, take a breath, count to three, and find a follow-up question instead. You might be surprised by just how much this simple shift can, well, shift things.

So, let's go ahead and give it a try—paying closer attention, probing gently, acknowledging generously, and facilitating clearly. Who knows what wonders lie on the other side of your next conversation?

Practical Exercise

So, you wanna get the lowdown on crafting *effective systemic questions*, huh?erfect, I'm here to walk you through a pretty cool exercise. Just you and me, strolling, through this jungle of rhetoric together. Fasten your metaphorical seatbelts; it's not as rough as a quiz night question, I promise.

First thing's first, **what in the world are systemic questions?** In the simplest terms, they're the kind that aim to get a deep understanding of a situation or problem by considering the whole system - like looking at the forest, not just oogling one particularly charming tree. These questions avoid yes/no dead-ends and encourage thinking and discussions that reveal connections and possibilities. (Sounds like detective work, but fancier, eh?)

Here's how we're gonna tackle learning about these bad boys, step-by-step:

Step 1: Gather Your Tools

You'll need something to write with, and on. Yeah, digital's cool, but there's something about pen and paper that just feels right. Makes you feel like an old-school scholar or something.

Step 2: Warm-up – "Tell me about a time..."

Let's get those gears turning. Think about a conversation you had that left you smiling ear to ear. What made it good? Was it the questions, the answers, the back and forth? Scribble your thoughts. No worries about neatness or sounding smart; this is just for you.

Step 3: Enter the World of Systemic Questions

Now, create a fictional, yet somewhat plausible, scenario in your life. Maybe it's trying to figure out why your study habits aren't leading to better grades, or why the vibe in your online gaming group feels off lately. The catch? You're playing detective, and you want the big picture.

Step 4: Craft Those Questions

For your chosen scenario, write out at least 5 systemic questions. Remember, we're not looking for "Did I study enough?" types. Nope, we're aiming for more like, "How does the way I organize my study time influence my test results?" Feel the difference? It's a little detail, but it pack a punch.

Step 5: Reflection Time

Alrighty, look back at the questions you wrote. **Do they prompt you to think deeper? Could these lead to a conversation with insights,* maybe even eureka moments?**ote what worked and what kinda... fell flat.

Step 6: Swap and Chat

Here's where things get juicy. Trade questions with a friend and talk them over. Notice how their perspective might offer new angles on your situation. This is the magic of systemic questions; they open doors, sometimes ones you didn't even realize were there.

And that's how you do it. Through this simple exercise - which, let's be honest, kinda feels like undercover detective work - you're not just asking questions. Nah, you're crafting keys that unlock doors to understanding complex systems. It's all about seeing the bigger picture, something we often forget in our go, go, go world.

Before signing off, a personal reflection: Asking better questions is a skill, no two ways about it. And like any skill, it demands practice.

Sometimes, you'll nail it; other times... it'll be a learning curve. But, every question is a step forward, shaping you into a more thoughtful, aware individual... or at least a pretty good conversation-starter at parties.

Keep curious. The art of asking questions never gets old—it just gets better and more intriguing.

Chapter 3: Implementing Systemic Questions in Leadership

So... we're wading into some deep waters here—and, yeah, let me be the first to say, it feels a bit like walking through a thick fog at times. You see, slapping the word "leadership" on anything instantly amps up the pressure, doesn't it? But let's take a step back, take a deep breath... and let's chat.

Leadership—isn't it quite the buzz around town? Yet, when we strip away all the glitter, at its heartbeat, it's about those precious moments of connection, of genuine, "Hey, how are you?" kind of talks. That's where "systemic questions" waltz in. Sounds fancy, I know—but stick with me.

In a nutshell, it's about asking questions... the kind that digs a little deeper (without turning into an awkward, prying session, of course). It's like, instead of asking your team, "Did you get the job done?" It's more along the lines of, "What new insights did you gain while working on this?" See the difference?

(Pause for a second—because if you're anything like me, right about now, you're thinking... Well, isn't this just good conversation skills 101? And, yeah, you'd be right to wonder.)

But here's the twist. Implementing these kinds of questions strategically in leadership has this almost magic-like quality. It's not just about making others feel seen or heard—but rather, truly engaging with their thought processes, their ideas, and even, their dilemmas.

And listen, I've had my fair share of eye-roll moments when topics seem all about "Let me fix you with my remarkable leadership skills." That's not what this chapter is. It's sharing some stories, shedding light on those moments when a simple question sparked an idea, lead to a breakthrough, or admittedly, fell flat—because, let's face it, not every swing is a hit.

So, what do you say? Let's explore this together, getting a feel for how just the right question, at just the right time, can indeed shift the tides—without needing to crack open a fortune-cooked-sized manual on how to be a "better leader". Yeah, I promise, no dull lectures here—just real talk, a sprinkle of humor, and perhaps, an insightful question or two that might just tickle your curiosity neurons.

Leadership and The Art of Strategic Inquiry

When you think about leadership, what comes to mind? Is it about giving orders, making decisions, and setting directions? Or is it something more? What if I were to say, it's about asking the right questions at the right time? Sounds simple, right? But believe me, it can be a game-changer.

Leadership isn't just about having all the answers... it's about **encouraging critical thinking** by developing capacities for "inquiring systems." This means shifting from a problem-solving orientation to strategic questioning. Now, I know what you're thinking, "What's the big difference?" It's like this - **solving a problem** is fixing something that's broken; asking strategic questions is about interpreting the situation in a new way that might open up unforeseen solutions or opportunities.

To put this into practice, creating an infrastructure for **dialogue and engagement** is a must, including reward systems that enhance cross-organizational collaboration. Imagine a workplace where everyone feels they can contribute ideas and question the status quo, without fear of retribution. Yep, it requires bold steps and, sometimes, a **leap of faith**.

"Leadership is not about being in charge. It's about taking care of those in your charge."

Finding and asking the right questions helps in, well, not just staying afloat in a volatile environment but actually charting a meaningful course. It demands that one stays endlessly **curious** – think of it as keeping your inner child alive, always asking "but why?"

"The smart leader's job is to create an environment where ideas are welcomed, tested, and implemented."

So, how do you, as a leader, start planting the seeds of this **inquiring and open culture** in which everyone is a contributor?

- Challenge **existing beliefs** by asking, "What are we assuming here that might not be true?"
- When faced with **a dilemma**, instead of jumping to conclusions, ask, "What alternatives haven't we considered?"
- Welcome moments of **failure or unforeseen outcomes** by pondering, "What can we learn from this that could guide us in the future?"

The notion of **strategic questioning** involves digging beneath the surface. Let's say a project missed a deadline... The easy route is to find who or what to blame. **Strategic Inquiry**, however, compels a deeper dive: "What processes, understanding, or communication could we improve to prevent a similar situation?"

It fosters a kind of conversation that's not always comfortable but invariably **growth-inducing**. Curiosity can make people a bit uneasy, granted... like when you're the odd one questioning why things are done a certain way. But here's the thing – **that's where innovation starts**.

Suddenly, you're not just managing teams to do things the right way, but leading them to discover what might lie beyond the immediate horizon. Here's something personal... once upon a time, in the hustle of achieving targets, I overlooked the **power of pause**, to reflect and inquire,

Implementing this doesn't happen overnight. It calls for patience, earnest effort, and, perhaps most **critically**, a willing shift of perspective both from the leadership and the team. I suggest small, continuous steps, reflective sessions, and shared storytelling events to breed this culture.

So, why not swap the hat of an all-knowing leader with that of a curious guide on a shared exploration? Your goal is to make everyone around you smarter with every question posed and every answer sought. Your path forward is defined not by the footprints behind but by the questions you dare to ask up ahead. Lead on!

Empowering Teams Through Thoughtful Questions

Empowering teams isn't about giving them answers... it's about asking the right questions. See, it's all about hitting the **sweet spot** of encouraging strategic thinking without directing it. You want to provoke thought, insight, and initiative. To do this, nothing beats a good mix of lineal and open-ended questions.

When we apply this in leadership, our aim shifts from providing solutions to stimulating a culture of curiosity and innovation. Instead of saying "Do it this way," we begin asking "What if we tried this?" or "How could we approach this differently?" It's a subtle change in language, but it makes a world of difference.

Take, for instance, the idea of encouraging innovation. When you lead with curious inquiry rather than direct advice, you open up a Pandora's box of creativity. Leaders who master this form of questioning understand that to really foster innovation, they sometimes need to step back... It allows the room necessary for groundbreaking ideas to surface.

"The future belongs to the curious... The ones who are not afraid to try it, question it, push it, flip it, turn it inside out, and upside down."

Another cornerstone is strategic questioning to reinforce organizational goals alignment. By posing reflective yet strategic questions, leaders remind everyone of the bigger picture. Here's a classic: "How does this project align with our core values and long-term objectives?" Simple, yet hugely revealing.

Problem-solving is another area where the subtle art of questioning can have a tremendous impact. Process-interruption and hypothesis questions can be particularly effective. Asking, "What happens if we stop this midway?" or "What evidence do we have to support this assumption?" directs focus to the problem's root, promoting a deeper level of understanding.

"Questions are the breath of life for a conversation."

Let me give you an anecdote to illustrate just how impactful thoughtful questioning can be. A leader in a tech company once told me how she turned around a project headed for doom. Instead of outlining a rescue plan, she asked her team, "How can we break this pattern?" This simple question challenged her team to think differently and, ultimately, led them to develop an ingenious solution.

So how can you, as a leader, make strategic questioning part of your regime? Here are a few tips:

- Always start with 'What' or 'How'. These are your **golden keys** to open-ended questions.
- Encourage follow-ups. When a team member asks a question, ask another question in return instead of providing an answer immediately.
- Celebrate all answers jotted down. This will reinforce the notion that it's not just about asking questions but pondering and reflecting on them together.

Incorporating thoughtful questioning into your leadership style can genuinely transform the dynamics of your team. It can move your team from being merely participants to active contributors -- crafting an atmosphere ripe for innovation, synergy, and unparalleled growth. So, next time you're in a team meeting, resist the urge to provide all the answers. Instead, harness the power of questions, and witness the magic unfold. Trust me, the results might just surprise you.

Welcoming a Culture of Curiosity and Innovation

In the world of leadership, stepping away from conventional frameworks and welcoming a culture of curiosity and innovation can make all the difference. It starts with painting the big picture— yes—that critical step where we zoom out to visualize the **entire landscape** of challenges and opportunities lying ahead and around. This is where systemic thinking sways into the scene, transforming complex challenges into easier roads leading to impactful solutions.

But how does one implement this with a team or clientele begging for clarity in a maze of systematic complexities? It's all about the types of questions you ask... and when you ask them. Mapping questions have become my secret weapon of choice. Picture this: you're facilitating a session, and instead of doling out directives, you're there weaving questions that make everyone stop and think about how they're influenced by the environments they're embedded in. These aren't your run-of-the-mill questions. No, they are designed to make clients and team members pinpoint exactly where they stand and how they're interconnected with the bigger picture.

"In a room full of experts, the most powerful tool is the right question."
"Through asking, we open doors that were never locked."

Circular coaching questions follow suit, serving a twin purpose. Firstly, they ignite a **collective awareness** within teams, stimulating a sense of unity and shared objectives. And, let's face it, this shared vision is the breeding ground for innovation. Secondly, such questions carve paths for honest, open conversations. We're talking about diminishing those towering walls of mistrust and fears, laying down the groundwork for a culture riddled with transparency and mutual respect.

So, what tacks should you take?

- Aiming to sense-feel-understand the underlying patterns.
- Stirring personal reflections to unmask those often overlooked internal and external influences.
- Opening avenues for shared narratives.

Exporting one from my collection of tales, I once led a team plagued by silos and fractional efforts, sounding all too familiar? I bet. The transformation began with systems mapping, piquing interest through curious inquiries about everyone's position and views within the larger goal we were tackling. This not only lubricated the gears for smoother collaborations but also erected an innovation-propelling greenhouse.

Example Exercises for the Bold Leaders:

- Craft a "Question of the Day" board in the workspace to spotlight mapping or circular questions, influencing daily reflections and interdisciplinary minglings.
- Encourage storytelling sessions where projects are dissected, inviting everyone to contribute their angle or how they see their threads running through the project fabric, enriching the collective tapestry of understanding and co-creation.

(Can I add a reflective sidenote here? Don't shy away from threading personal stories or light-hearted anecdotes into your leadership approach. It adds that taste of humanity and relatability that pure data and structured methodologies occasionally lack.)

A common pitfall many leaders tumble into is locking themselves within the confines of authority, missing out on the dynamism user-centric questions can incubate. Placing subjects—be it clients or team members—within the circles and cycles of their environment rather than on distant pedestals enhances connectivity, empathy, and ultimately, innovation.

And, no need to fret over perfection here. It's the strides toward cultivating a questioning mindset paired with zestful curiosity that flowers into the biggest feats. Keep those inquiry gears oiled, keep the approachability alive, and watch as you steer your vessel through the challenges, not just as a commander but as a curious co-navigator seeking the treasures of insights and innovation together.

Addressing Challenges and Conflicts with Questions

When stepping into the art of **leadership**, one quickly learns that challenges and conflicts aren't roadblocks but rather gateways to growth and better team dynamics, if – and that's a big if – you approach them with the right mindset.

Say you're faced with a **stubborn opposition** from a team member or a full-blown crisis within your project team. You might feel your first instinct is to dive (sorry, focus!), dictate terms, and provide solutions. But what if I told you there's a more, let's say, elegant way to dance around these conflicts? It involves **asking smart, strategic questions**.

Let's break it down. The crux of dealing with opposition or skepticism lies in:

- Encouraging new possibilities through directive and instructive strategic questions,
- Employing curiosity while responding to resistance or objections,
- Utilizing reframing techniques when addressing opposition,
- And maintaining an emotionally intelligent mindset that balances both individual and team interests.

I know what you're thinking, "Easier said than done, right?" Fair point, but bear with me.

Encouragement of new possibilities isn't just **wishful thinking**. It's about directing the team's focus toward unexplored avenues. Here's a story: once during a particularly heated team meeting, where the air was practically electric with opposing views, I decided to ask, "What haven't we tried yet that could actually turn this around?" The room went silent, not because I asked something profound, but because it shifted the dynamic. People started thinking **constructively** rather than defensively.

"It's not about having the right answers but asking the right questions."

Curiosity is your best friend. That's hard to internalize, especially when every fiber of you wants to defend your point. Responding to **objections** with genuine curiosity can go like, "I see you're unconvinced about this approach. What concerns you the most?" This shows respect and an open stance to understand and **acknowledge**.

In the maze of leadership and teamwork, reframing is your **compass**. Imagine someone says, "This is impossible; we can't meet that deadline." Instead of conceding or worse, forcing a "Yes, we can," try, "What needs to happen for us to get closer to the deadline, even if we can't meet it fully?" It's not just changing "can't" to "can"; it's about expanding the **frame** from "impossible" to "Let's work with what we have."

"Every problem is an opportunity in disguise."

Emotional intelligence, ah, the real MVP here! Keeping cool and balancing interests, essentially means you're acknowledging, without saying it out loud, "I hear you, and you're valued." Simple in theory, complex in practice, yet incredibly rewarding.

Here's a **golden rule**: never put someone on the spot or force anyone into a corner. The minute you do, defenses go up, and productivity goes down. Instead, approach every challenge or conflict with a blend of curiosity, strategy, guidance, and empathy. A tall order? Maybe. But imagine the alternatives – yep, not pretty.

In rounding off, implementing systemic questions in leadership doesn't just transform how you address **challenges and conflicts**; it kind of revolutionizes it. Cue your efforts in encouraging possibilities, reframing issues, and promoting emotional intelligence. Then watch, not just wait, actively watch as your team starts to gel, grow, and overcome obstacles not because they have to but because they've been led to see them as nothing more than stepping stones. Dear reader, **the ball is truly in your court**, and may those questions flow effortlessly!

Sustaining Growth and Learning in Teams

Got a moment? Let's get right to it. When you're leading a pack, questions aren't just questions. They're the keys to unlocking doors to streets less traveled, where collaboration dances with progress. Now, let me walk you through the alleys where effective solutions meet quality management excellence. Think of managing not just as directing but nurturing a garden where accountability is the water, and admitting mistakes is the sunlight. "Mistakes," they say, "are the stepping stones to learning." Rectifying errors proactively makes the path smoother for everyone.

Respecting stakeholders is another critical chapter in this quest. Imagine walking a mile in their shoes, listening intently, valuing every nugget of input, addressing worries head-on. Sounds straightforward, right? Yet it often gets overlooked in the bustling corridors of leadership. Actively listening polishes the mirror, reflecting not just what's said, but also what's left unsaid...

So, how does this all tie into nurturing a **continuous learning and innovation culture**? Simple, you spice up the routine with **smart systemic questions**. A fertile ground for growth demands routines that question, challenge, and inspire. Here are a few examples to grease the wheels:

- "What did we learn today that surprised us?"
- "How can we make this mistake into a valuable lesson?"
- "In what unique ways can we leverage each team member's strengths?"

These aren't your run-of-the-mill queries. No, sir. They invite digging deeper, going beyond the regrets of "what's done is done." They favor brains storming together, clashing, converging, emerging with something new. They cradle respect, foster dialogue, and above all, declare an open season on creative solutions and self-reflection.

Ah, but let me sidetrack just a bit—because there's something that doesn't quite get the spotlight it deserves. The power of **admitting you don't know everything**. Yeah, I said it. Presenting yourself as the oracle of everything can backfire. It's like saying you've read every book ever written. Impossible, right? Here's a nugget of truth:

"The best leaders are those who know the power hidden in the vulnerability of not knowing."

It creates space for others to step in, contribute, and form trust. It transforms an individual quest into a crusade, rallying the troops behind a shared vision.

And speaking of shared visions, it's your torchbearer. It expresses that looking ahead together, team members will rally, innovate, and surge forward. Here's another axiom you might appreciate:

"Powerful questions nurture aspiration; they sculpt out of the mundane the very essence of hope and actionable paths."

A balanced mix of short sprints and long relay races, smart systemic questioning is not the usual way. Remember though, as seriously as we take our strides and fall, this whole affair? It's sprinkled with bouts of laughter, eye rolls at snafus, and the rare elegance of creating things anew. And perhaps, just perhaps, in these moments of truth and dare, of trial and error, lie the seeds for the next big bloom.

It's all there, laid bare as a tableau - lead with humility, craft a learning symphony, keep your ear to the ground, and who knows, the rhythm just might catch on. Let it be known, tomorrow begins with the questions we dare to ask today. And as for mistakes, promote them like old friends, for without them, perfection's story remains untold.

Leadership Reflections: Self-Inquiry for Personal Growth

When we think about leadership, we often envision someone at the helm, guiding a team through the highs and lows of a project or the life of a company. It seems like such a straightforward thing... if only it really were. In the everyday hustle, what often gets lost is the power of reflection—particularly, self-inquiry for personal growth. This isn't about merely asking yourself how your day went; it's about probing deeper... into the *why*, the *how*, and the impacts of your actions.

Self-reflection can be a tad scary, I won't lie. It's easier to critique another's actions than to turn the lens on ourselves. But here's a thing

I've found—there's **immense growth in discomfort**. The practices and mind-sets inherited over the years mold our leadership style in ways we don't even notice. It's only when we pause, when we ask the *right* questions, that some of these patterns reveal themselves for observation, questioning, and—hopefully—improvement.

For instance, I once found myself wrestling with this piercing question during a leadership retreat:

"What are the values that I stand for, and how do my actions as a leader showcase these values?"

Pondering over this, I penned down virtues important to me—integrity, creativity, and empathy, to name a few. These weren't just words to adorn a wall in the office. These were the guiding stars for my interactions with my team, decisions I took... the very culture I strived to cultivate within the group. Once laid bare, I could see—with uncomfortable clarity—areas where my actions hadn't quite matched up to these ideals.

Another reflection exercise that stirred the pot went something like this;

"How would my team describe my leadership in my absence?"

Now, **that** question could entail some heart-thumping moments. Yet, entertaining such introspection inspired authentic conversations—assertions of what works alongside constructive feedback. Such conversations are treasures—they build trust and open channels of communication heretofore possibly ignored.

So, how do you, dear reader, initiate this transformative journey of self-inquiry? Here's a simple breakdown:

- Set aside time regularly for reflection. Valuing this practice is the first step.
- Jot down your actual experiences as a leader; specifics often reveal more than vagaries.

- Ask yourself hard questions. Reflect on both your victories and times you fell short.
- Welcome feedback from others. This **mirror** to your actions can shape your journey profoundly.

(- Remember, it's a loop of continual growth, not just a one-off exercise.)

Leadership phenom John C was quoted as saying, "Everything rises and falls on leadership". So true. Real growth and development take root not just in acquiring new skills but in the fertile soil of self-reflection and -understanding. As a leader, paving the way forward for not just your team, but yourself in terms of personal growth and adherence to your core values, could be the most pivotal stride you make—impacting not only your career, but the lives radiating around it. So, next time you're sipping on your morning coffee or tea, before the day claims you, ponder... Reflect... What question will you ask yourself today?

Practical Exercise

Alright, let's get down to brass tacks. The thing I'm about to throw your way is all about **Chapter 3: Implementing Systemic Questions in Leadership.** Imagine you're the coach, the MVP in the field of leadership or consulting, and your playground is the complex, sometimes chaotic world of business organizations. Your goal? To become a wizard at asking these powerful systemic questions that can unravel (in a good way) the Gordian knots your clients are facing.

Step 1: Brush Up on the Basics

First thing's first, you gotta know what you're working with. If you're not already familiar, get yourself *acquainted* with the foundation of systemic thinking. I'm talking about understanding that everything in an organization is connected, like spaghetti in a bowl. There's no linear "this causes that," but rather a web of actions and reactions. So, pull out your notes from **"The Systemic Guide to Coaching"**. or was it a book? Yeah, skim through that.

Step 2: Question Crafting

Next up, let's craft some questions but not just any questions — we're talking about those that make people **pause** and think, "Hm, I've never looked at it that way before." These questions should help your clients see the patterns, the relationships, and the dynamics at play in their organization. Think along the lines of, "What happens when..." or "How do changes in... affect...?" And, I mean, feel free to toss in a bit of humor or lightness to your process; sometimes it's the unexpected that brings insight.

Step 3: Role-Play

This is where the rubber meets the road. Pair up with a buddy — yes, I said buddy because we're keeping things casual here. Each of you takes turns being the leader facing a complex situation in their phantom organization. Use your newfound questioning powers to explore the system. Go wild with it. I mean, not too wild, but let the creativity flow.

Step 4: Reflection Time

After your role-play shenanigans, huddle up and reflect. What did you notice about the process? Did any of the questions lead to an 'a-ha' moment? It's all about learning and tweaking your approach, making sure you're pulling at the right threads to get a clear *picture* of the challenge at hand.

Step 5: Take It to the Streets

Alrighty, time to put it into action in the wild, wild world. Next time you're in a session with a client, introduce one or two systemic questions into the conversation. Observe their response, and adapt as necessary. Remember, this is a *learning process;* perfection is not the goal but progress.

So, dear coach, leader, or consultant, ready to sharpen your systemic questioning skills and tackle those organizational knots? Think of it as adding a shiny new tool to your toolbox — one that could really make a difference. Plus, it's a nice way to show off at the next industry meet-up. Just saying.

And, as you're working through this exercise, remember to give yourself a pat on the back. It's not easy stepping into new territory, but hey, look at you doing the thing! Keep pushing, and who knows, maybe you'll be writing the next **big hit book** in your niche about systemic thinking. How cool would that be?

Chapter 4: Systemic Questions for Improved Communication Skills

So... we're diving into a chapter that's really close to my heart. Why, you ask? Well, think about those times when words just slipped out wrong, and your intentions were lost in translation. Yeah, we've all been there. This chapter focuses on systemic questions - a fancy term, I know, but stick with me here! These are questions designed, quite cleverly, might I add, to improve how we interact with each other. You see, it's not only about asking better questions, but about opening up a whole new world of understanding each other. Cool, huh?

(Can I be honest for a sec? As a teen, my communication skills were, let's just say, less than stellar. I would've given anything for a guide like this. Just saying.)

It's fascinating how psychology plays into this. Ever notice how when someone truly gets where you're coming from, it almost feels like they read your mind? That's the power of asking the right questions. It shows we're listening—not just hearing the words, but really processing what's behind them. And sure, it may feel a bit awkward at first, pivoting your question-asking strategy, if you will. But, I promise, it gets more natural.

Throughout this chapter, I invite you to ponder over reflections like, "Huh, why didn't I think of that before?" or even, "Could this, perhaps, make me a wizard at conversations?" We're tackling this with a mix of humor, some light-hearted examples, and...yes, personal anecdotes – because, why not? We're all friends here, exploring this tricky business of human interaction.

By the end of this journey together, my hope is that you'll start seeing conversations differently. Not just exchanges of words, but as opportunities (there's that lovely word) to truly connect, understand, and maybe even leave someone thinking, "Wow, that was a great chat!" So, dear reader, ready to get started? (No need to answer that. It's rhetorical. But hey, enthusiasm is appreciated!)

Listening Actively for Deeper Understanding

So, how do we *really listen* to elevate our conversations and relationships? Well, let me break it down, starting with the basics like summarizing and paraphrasing what the other person says. Yep, that's right. It's about repeating their message in your own words, making sure you've caught the right drift. It isn't just repeating their words like a parrot; it's showing you're trying, I mean **really trying** to get where they're coming from.

When someone is talking, ever notice how a simple nod, eye contact, or leaning a bit forward can make the whole difference? These aren't just random actions. They're nonverbal cues that scream (quietly, of course), "I'm with you, I'm listening." And trust me, the person speaking can feel that energy. It's like they say:

"The most basic and powerful way to connect to another person is to listen. Just listen."

Reflection is another gem in our toolkit. It goes a bit like this: You listen, and then you kinda play it back in a "this is what I'm hearing, does that sound right?" way. It's not mimicking. It's more like checking if your ears and their mouth are on the same page, especially when it comes to emotions and perceptions.

Empathy, oh empathy. This is where you dig deep and acknowledge those feelings and emotions bubbling up in the conversation. Not in a casual "Yeah, I hear what you're saying" but in an "I see you" way. You're recognizing and validating their feelings, like giving them a big verbal hug.

Here's a little story to tie it all together. A friend of mine was struggling with feeling overlooked at work. I practiced **active listening**, absorbing every word, nodding, keeping that eye contact strong. Then, I used a **reflection statement**, something like, "Sounds like you're feeling invisible when your efforts don't get acknowledged." And finally, I tapped into **empathy** by adding, "That must be tough, feeling like you're not making an impact." The relief on their face – it was like a weight had been lifted, all because I chose to *listen with intent.*

To get you started, why not practice these steps in your next conversation:

- Summarize what the other person has said,
- Use nonverbal cues to show engagement,
- Reflect their statements,
- Acknowledge their feelings.

"Listening is an art that requires attention over talent, spirit over ego, others over self."

Don't get me wrong, mastering these techniques takes time. It's not going to be an overnight transformation, but progress, oh sweet progress, does come (*cue the triumphant background music*). You'll notice differences, tiny at first – deeper connections, more meaningful conversions, and before you know it, boom, you're not halfway bad at this whole listening thing.

Before wrapping this up, let's have a heart-to-heart. Upping your listening game isn't just about improving *how* you speak to others. It's about transforming the quality of your communications and, by extension, your relationships. Shoot, it might just change small bits of the world around you. So, give these approaches a go, flex that listening muscle, and watch the magic unfurl in your conversations. And hey, enjoying the process is all part of the fun.

Building Rapport through Empathetic Questioning

Isn't it amazing, the power of a well-placed question? It's like, the moment you toss out a "How do you feel about that?" or "What's behind your thinking on that?", the whole dynamic of a conversation can change. Now, I'm not saying this is some sort of magic bullet, but it does work wonders in getting folks to open up more than they might with just your run-of-the-mill chitchat.

When we lean into questions that start with "what", "how", or "can you explain", we're doing more than just fishing for information. We're showing the speaker we're genuinely interested in what they have to say. This kind of deep communication can't help but lead to stronger connections. And who doesn't want that?

Here's a quick story: last Tuesday, I sat down with a colleague, Alice, who seemed a bit off. Instead of prying with a brusque "What's wrong?", I opted for a gentler, "How has your day been affecting you?" Notice the difference? It was like opening a door— she shared her challenges, and through that sharing, I learned so much more not just about her situation but about how she deals with pressure.

"To truly listen is to risk being changed forever."

There's a kind of poetry in that line, one that reminds us that communicating isn't just about transferring information. It's about allowing ourselves to be moved by the stories of others. And let me tell you, reflecting those stories back...that's gold. Saying things like, "So, what I hear you saying is..." or "It sounds like you're feeling..."; they make the speaker feel **validated**. Like their words are worth weighing and considering. And believe me, feeling heard is half the battle in feeling understood.

Let's get down to this - **Empathy.** Now if there were ever a secret sauce in building rapport, this is it. When you inject phrases like "I understand how that could be tough", or "that does sound challenging", it's remarkable how it bridges gaps. You aren't agreeing or disagreeing, merely honoring their sentiment.

Above all? Listen. Just listen. Don't jump in with an interjection or bolt towards giving advice. The gold is in letting the other person complete their thoughts. It tells them, "Hey, I value what you have to say, and I'm here for you." Isn't that a beautiful thing, when you stop to think about it?

"Questions are the breath of life for a conversation."

Ever found yourself stuck—in a dialogue where yes and no answers kill the mood faster than a snowball in summer? Here's a trick: consciously shift to open-ended questions. Not only do they provide the person room to express themselves, but they also demonstrate your interest in a **deepen dialogue.**

Here's an exercise: next time you're having a tea, coffee, or even just a moment with someone, practice tossing out one open-ended query. Notice the change in how they respond, not just with their words, but with the openness of their body language and the brightness in their eyes. It's compelling, how simple shifts in how we question can transform exchanges from mundane to meaningful.

So, as we keep stepping forward, our path twists and turns with countless opportunities to bind, to mingle, to grasp the stories untold waiting in the eager breath of our next query. Let's be bold, let's celebrate curiosity, and above all, let's genuinely listen. With every question, we're not just talking—we're tethering worlds together, one conversation at a time.

Face Difficult Conversations with Ease

Who hasn't found themselves sweating, maybe a bit, during a tough chat? You know the ones. They're often needed yet dreaded—the kind where the stakes feel sky-high, and so does the tension. So, let's roll up our sleeves and get into how to glide through these conversations a bit more smoothly, using **smart systemic questions** and a hefty dose of **positive psychology**.

First things first, doing your homework pays off. Have you ever walked into a tricky dialogue only to be smacked with an objection you didn't see coming? Ouch, right? Here's a better plan: before you find yourself in the hot seat, try to anticipate the tough questions and possible objections. Sketch them out. Think about your responses. It's like having a map in unknown territory.

Now, remember the power of those two little letters: **"I"**. When things get prickly, nobody likes feeling accused. Swapping out "you" accusations for "I" statements is like a conversation superhero move. For real. It shifts the vibe from blame to understanding. "I felt overlooked in yesterday's meeting," packs a different punch than, "You overlooked me." See what I mean?

And speaking of punches... **don't throw them. (Metaphorically speaking, of course.)** We're focusing on the issue here, not attacking the person. It's incredibly easy to blur these lines when emotions are high. But trust me, chopping at the issue without making it personal? That's where the magic happens.

"Assertiveness is not about building a fortress around your point of view, but bridging the gap between yours and others."

What assertiveness does is it lets you stand your ground, while also being a decent human being. How? By expressing your thoughts and feelings honestly—and this is key—while listening and truly acknowledging those of others. It's not a monologue; it's a dialogue. Simple? Sure. Easy? Maybe not so much, but worth it.

For example, you could say, "I'm committed to improving our workflow. I felt frustrated that our meeting didn't touch on possible

61

solutions. I'd like to understand your perspective more." Here, you're owning your feelings, proposing forward movement, and inviting participation. It's assertive, yet respectful.

Let's toss in some real-life practice. Maybe you're dealing with a relentless curveball-tosser at work. Instead of plotting their defeat in your 4 p.m. daydream, approach them. And remember—this isn't Gladiator; it's more like a friendly game of table tennis. Breathe, be present, and...

- Take a moment to sort your thoughts before you speak
- Share your intentions clearly
- Use "I" statements
- Listen... I mean, really, truly listen

In these conversations, realizing we are all humans scrambling to do our best (usually, anyway) creates a strong platform to connect from.

"Through empathy and assertiveness, find a shared path forward."

Remember what we've talked about here. It's not about winning; it's about moving forward together. Knowing when to be silent can often speak volumes. And surprise, surprise... sometimes, asking a well-placed question can shift the battleground to common ground.

Facing difficult conversations with skill and ease requires practice, patience, and a genuine consideration for the perspectives of others. So next time you find yourself at the edge of one of these daunting chats, take a deep breath... You've got an arsenal now. Use it wisely, and, who knows, maybe these conversations end up a bit more on the **easy** side.

Breaking Down Barriers to Clear Communication

So, what's the big deal about breaking down barriers to clear communication? Well, for starters, clear communication is like the golden ticket in both our personal and professional lives. It's what helps us get our points across effectively and can really make the difference in achieving our goals. Now, let's get into some of the nitty-gritty on how we can tackle those pesky barriers.

First things first, confusing concepts and terminology. Ever been in a meeting and someone starts throwing around jargon like it's going out of style? It's like, slow down there, buddy...what does that even mean? It's crucial to "clarify confusing concepts and terminologies that may hinder clear communication". Because, let's face it, we're not all walking dictionaries.

When chatting or emailing, I always try to simplify complex ideas. It's like, if something can be said in five words instead of fifty, I'm all for it. The simpler, the better. And, if you've got to use that fancy jargon, maybe throw in a quick explanation too. Just a friendly heads-up can do wonders. It's all about ensuring everyone's on the same page, because, otherwise, we might as well be speaking different languages.

Next up, dialogue. I can't stress enough how asking open-ended questions can change the game. Here, let me give you an example:

"What do you think about implementing this strategy in our next project? Do you see any risks or benefits that we should discuss?"

Notice how that invites a dialogue instead of just saying, "Do this task," which pretty much shuts down any room for a productive conversation. People like to feel heard, not commanded. It's about creating a space where ideas can flow freely.

Now, here's a biggie: **constructive feedback.** It's like walking a tightrope, balancing on that thin line between being helpful and coming off as...well, not so helpful. The magic formula? Point out what's working well, highlight areas for improvement, and

encourage. Always encourage. Feedback isn't about pointing fingers; it's about **growth** and support. Like, imagine saying:

"I really appreciate how you tackled the budgeting issue in your report. Have you considered incorporating more current diagrams to help illustrate your points? I believe this could make your argument even stronger."

See how it points out both a positive aspect and an area that can use a bit of upgrading—all without sounding like a know-it-all.

Remember, the goal here is to promote understanding and **growth.** Language plays a huge part in that. Keep it **clear, concise,** and above all, **kind.**

To sum it all up, effective communication isn't rocket science, but it does require a bit of mindfulness—paying attention not just to what we say, but how we say it...because at the end of the day, we all want to be understood. Life's all about learning and adapting, so let's keep the dialogue rolling, simplifying where we can, and building each other up. After all, isn't that what communication is all about?

The Role of Feedback in Effective Exchange

When we talk, it's all about the vibe, right? So, when someone tosses over feedback, it's a bit like catching a frisbee. You've gotta be ready, aim well, and throw it back with equal precision. First up, always remember to offer feedback **promptly**—I mean as soon as you notice something worth mentioning. Why, you ask? Well, it's kinda like trying to recall what you had for breakfast last week; the details get fuzzy unless it was something really standout.

Now, onto the nitty-gritty. You're going to want to use **specific examples** rather than making broad, sweeping statements. > "When you gave that presentation, I noticed you engaged with the audience by asking interactive questions. That really kept everyone on their toes and attentive." Notice how it's clear, precise, and doesn't beat around the bush?

Another golden rule is to focus on **observable behavior. We're talking about what you can see and hear, not the guesses or interpretations buzzing around in your head.** So **instead of saying, "I feel like you're not interested in this project,"** you **could try, "I've noticed you've been missing a lot of our scheduled meetings. Is everything OK?"**

Balance is key, kind of like that sweet spot between eating vegetables and the good stuff (chocolate). Same goes with feedback; you need a mix of positive and **constructive critiques.** Yeah, both sides of the coin. Trust me, it helps keep people motivated and not feel like they're under a microscope.

Now, about those feedback sessions, they're a little like playing ping-pong. You lob over a critique, you better be ready for the ball to come back. So, prep yourself for a two-way street conversation:

- Positives first, like, "I really appreciated how thorough your report was."
- Add in a sprinkle of, "I think including more current statistics could give it an extra edge."

And then, don't just stand there! Encourage a bit of back-and-forth, get their take on things. Could make a whole lot of difference.

"Feedback is only as good as the action that follows. Keep it open, keep it honest, and make it timely."

Throw in a bit of personal reflection, why don't ya? Like a time you got some feedback that really opened your eyes. Funny thing is, we often see our mishaps as mere blips, while someone else can spot a pattern. Fascinating, right?

Lastly, keep that tone **conversational** and **personal**. No one likes feeling they're being lectured by a robot. Use those "I" statements, and maybe a dash of humor if you've got it. A chuckle here and there never hurt anybody. But listen, (seriously, lean in closer), this isn't about soft-pedaling or beating around the bush. It's about getting straight to the point, but doing it with some grace. So go ahead, give that feedback like you're serving up a gourmet meal – with care, attention, and a bit of flair. Who knows, it might just make all the difference in forming a **strong, effective communication.**

Advanced Techniques in Persuasive Communication

When we communicate, sometimes it feels like trying to get a cat to walk on a leash. Let me tell you, it's a lot more than just throwing words around and hoping something sticks.

Storytelling and **vivid descriptions** have this uncanny ability to pull people into your world. Ever found yourself so absorbed in a story that you forgot where you were? That's the power of emotional engagement. It's like... when you tell someone about your worst date ever, and they're hanging on every word, wide-eyed. It's real, it's raw, and it's relatable. *

"To effectively communicate, we must understand our audience passionately as if they were characters not outsourced by us by any means, but part and parcel of the story we breathe and live."

Now, let's chat about appearing credible — it's simpler than you may think. To be trusted, you gotta be consistent. Show up, keep to your word, and make sure your actions always match your speeches. It's like being that friend who's always there, rain or shine. Trustworthiness stems from, well, actually being reliable. Who would have thought, right?

So, about focusing on outcomes… People don't buy products; they buy **better versions of themselves**. It's not a drill you're selling; it's the hole it makes… or rather, the shelf that'll hang on that wall and what it represents - organization, style, and maybe even a happy partner. So, **benefits** — always have them at the front of your mind.

Now, onto the SCARF model. The acronym stands for:

- **Status** – Everyone wants to feel important, right?
- **Certainty** – We all appreciate a bit of predictability in our lives.
- **Autonomy** – Being in control of what happens to us is paramount.
- **Relatedness** – We're herd animals, folks. Connection is key.
- **Fairness** – Nobody likes feeling cheated.

This framework is like seasoning your grandma's secret recipe; use it wisely, and everyone will ask for seconds.

Did you ever wonder why some people can just, I don't know — get away with words, like they've got some sort of superpower? Here's a not-so-secret secret: **pause…** using emphatic gestures or pauses makes your speech engaging. It's not rocket science, but… **powerful.**

Exercise for the keen:

- Next time you're conversing with someone, consciously integrate a narrative into your dialogue. Notice their reaction. Maybe, "I had this dog, Jerry. Crooked tail, one eye bigger than the other, absolute dork. Guess what he did…" You've got a story; share it.

Now, welcoming these strategies might take practice. Don't go all in, throwing every technique at once. **Baby steps.**

*"The art of persuasion is learning not about manipulating but indeed sowing seeds of concepts **organically,** becoming the **guide on the side** rather than the sage on the stage."*

And remember, authentic communication isn't solely about what we say or how eloquently, (*I still can't get that story about Jerry off my mind, can you?*) we say it, but in ensuring our audience leaves feeling **engaged, satisfied,** and with a little more knowledge or insight than they arrived with. Think about it, isn't communication, after all, the art of being genuinely understood? So, **next time** you find yourself in a dialogue, maybe consider how your words, woven carefully, can truly **paint a picture** worth more than a thousand words.

Practical Exercise

Alright, let's dive--... let's get into a really cool exercise about **Chapter 4: Systemic Questions for Improved Communication Skills.** You might be wondering, "What on earth does that even mean?" Well, I'm here to guide you through this, step by casual step. Our goal? To make our conversations as meaningful as a home-cooked meal shared with old friends. Sounds good? Let's roll.

Step 1: Understand the Terrain

First off, let's get a grip on what systemic questions really are. In the simplest terms, they're **questions** that help you get to the heart of what someone is **thinking** or **feeling**. Why is this important, you ask? Because sometimes, we get stuck in our own heads and forget there's a whole other person with thoughts and feelings in the conversation.

Step 2: The Prep Work

Before you can dive... before you can start, you need a buddy for this exercise. Pick someone – a friend, a sibling, even your grandma (grandmas have endless wisdom, just so you know). Tell them that you're trying to better your communication skills and you'd love their help. More often than not, they'll be more than happy to assist. Who doesn't want smoother conversations?

Step 3: Crafting Your Questions

Here's where it starts getting a bit more interesting. Draft a list of open-ended questions. I'm talking about questions that can't be answered with a simple "yes" or "no". Questions like "What was the highlight of your day?" or "How did that situation make you feel?" Trust me, you're aiming for the kind of questions that make the other person pause and think, "Hmm, interesting question..."

Step 4: Putting It into Practice

Alright, it's go time. Sit down with your chosen person and start **engaging** in a conversation. Here's the trick, sprinkle in the questions you've crafted naturally into the conversation. Don't force them. Your goal is to encourage the other person to share more about their thoughts and feelings. And please, **please**, don't make it feel like an interrogation. This is key.

Step 5: Listen. Really Listen

This part is crucial. When they're responding to your questions, really **listen**. And I mean, truly be in the moment. Show that you're engaged by nodding, making eye contact, and responding appropriately. Remember, it's not just about waiting for your turn to speak. It's about walking a mile in their shoes (metaphorically, of course).

Step 6: Reflection

After the conversation has wound down, take a moment to reflect. Maybe jot down a few notes. Think about how those questions shifted the dynamic of the chat. Was it more interesting? Did you feel like you connected on a deeper level? Reflect on what worked, what didn't, and how you felt throughout the experience.

Alright, now here's a pro tip: don't be afraid to mix things up and try new questions in your next conversation. Communication, like any art, improves with practice and patience.

For extra credit, share your reflections with your partner in crime – the person you chose for this exercise. Discussing what you've both noticed and felt can open up another layer to enrich your communication skills even further. And, who knows? They might be keen to give it a try as well.

Before signing off, just a little **reflected thought** - remember, this whole exercise is not only about bettering your communication skills but also about connecting with people on a more genuine level. And in today's world, that's golden.

And there you have – not so daunting, right? Give it a go. You'd be surprised at how much a few well-thought-out questions can change a conversation. Good vibes and smooth talking!

Chapter 5: The Intersection of Positive Psychology and Systemic Inquiry

So, when I first bumped into the idea of blending positive psychology and systemic inquiry, I was like, "What in the world can these two topics offer each other?" It's kinda like finding out two of your friends from completely different circles actually know each other. Fascinating, right?

Now, diving into the heart of it, positive psychology isn't just about being happy or, you know, seeing the glass as half full—though, don't get me wrong, those bits help. It's more about understanding what really pushes our buttons, what makes us tick and, ultimately, what can lead us to living more fulfilling lives. On the flip side, systemic inquiry . . . well, it's a fancy way of saying we're looking at the big picture, how things link up and influence one another in complex systems.

Ever felt like no matter how much you break things down, you're missing something bigger? Yeah, me too. That's where this interesting combo comes in, sort of like peanut butter and jelly—unexpected but surprisingly delightful.

In this chapter, and don't worry, I'll keep it light, we're gonna stroll through how these two worlds collide. We'll look into how shifting our focus from what's wrong in our lives (thanks, traditional psych) to what's right can actually serve as an "aha" moment in seeing bigger patterns and playing nicer with the systems we live in.

We'll chat about stories, personal ones too because—let's be honest—if I bore you to tears, what's the point? My hopes are by the end, you're looking at things a tad differently, maybe even questioning. Like, isn't it curious how focusing on our strengths and positives can alter not just our outlook but the dynamics of groups, families, maybe even workplaces?

Oh, prepare yourself for some cheesy metaphors, random bursts of excitement, and maybe a few "Hmm, I never thought of it that way" moments as we as we go about this chapter. If there's one thing I've learned in life, it's that connections are everywhere, often hiding in plain sight. Let's discover some together!

Empowering Mindsets through Positive Questioning

When you think about **positive psychology** and **systemic inquiry**, things might seem a bit abstract, right? Let's weave these concepts into the cloth of everyday life – because, trust me, they're practical, and they can really change the way you see things...if you give them a chance. Do you surf the waves of affirmation and aspiration in your questioning? Or do you tend to find yourself stuck in the mud of negative assumption?

Affirmative topic creation isn't just a fancy phrase; it's like crafting the key that opens the door to aspiration exploration. Ever noticed how a change in the way a question is framed can completely transform the conversation? Picture this: Instead of asking "Why do we always struggle with this?", try "What can we do to improve?" You're essentially shifting from a **problem-centric** to a **solution-focused mindset.** And, boom – the whole mood changes.

Getting the atmosphere right is crucial... and that's where **humanized lead-ins** come into play. They're about making the setting right for open discussion – kind of like turning on the light in a room to make it inviting. It's all about making the other person feel at ease, seen, and ready to engage. Let's say you've got someone in your team, and you start off with, "I really loved your perspective on our last project... How do you think we can bring those ideas here?" Suddenly, the floor's theirs, and they're ready to contribute with a sunny disposition.

"The quality of our questions determines the quality of our answers."

Speaking of the craft of questioning, let's not overlook the power of **subquestions** during discussions. It's like looking at a gemstone from different angles – each reflection offers something unique. Subquestions help us uncover those multi-angle insights, providing a richer, fuller picture. You're delving, exploring the crevices of conversation that often get overlooked.

Now, let's yarn about **storytelling** – honestly, who doesn't like a good story? It's not just for amateurs; it's the golden ticket to engagement and connection. Stories weave the human element into discussions, like "Let me tell you about a time..." which naturally lowers defenses and fosters **human connections.** It's potent stuff, guys. Stories make the abstract tangible; they ground lofty ideas in the mud and leaves of real life.

"Storytelling is the bridge between connectivity and understanding."

The real kicker in transforming your approach is simple... yet profoundly effective:

- **Listen actively.** Yes, it's about questions, but it's also about creating the space to truly listen to the answers.
- Be bold enough to ask what others may shy away from – **personal reflections, feelings, aspirations.** These aren't just fluff; they're the guts of real communication.
- Encourage sharing by sharing... **Create a reciprocal environment.** You share a slice of your life, they share theirs – all of a sudden, you've got a meal going, not just disparate ingredients.

And yes, it's like a dance, mixing the beats and rhythm – a bit of systemic inquiry here, a splash of positive psychology there. Mash them up, and you've got this vibrant, soulful melody that draws people in and encourages them to think, to reflect. It's about unlocking doors without forcing them open, creating spaces that invite exploration and growth.

Keep in mind, these ideas aren't exhaustive. They're an invitation, spurring **creativity, inspiration,** and personal growth. By promoting positive questioning, we cultivate environments that nurture not just productive conversations but also **personal connections** and **deep insights** – all keys to top-notch communication and leadership.

Building Resilience with Constructive Inquiry

So, stepping right into the heart of it... Building resilience isn't exactly a walk in the park. But, guess what? It's totally achievable with some **smart thinking** and the right kind of **questions**. And no, I'm not talking about just any questions, but those that push us to look at challenges from a fresher perspective.

Let's break it down.

First up, tackling challenges positively is like having a toolkit that's always handy. Think about it... when life throws a curveball, what's your first move? Panic? Stress eat? Well, how about flipping the script and asking yourself, "What can I learn from this?" This simple shift in questioning can set a whole new tone on how we approach obstacles.

Now, onto acknowledging strengths – because, let's face it, we all have them, even if we occasionally forget. It's kind of like having a treasure chest but forgetting it's right under our bed. By recognizing what we're good at, we tap into a source of empowerment. "What have I done well today?" See, doesn't that question already make you feel a bit stronger?

"To know yourself is the beginning of wisdom."

Reflecting on past successes works wonders, too. It's easy to get bogged down by what's going wrong, causing us to forget all the mountains we've already climbed. Asking, "When have I successfully faced a similar situation?" helps keep our motivation for future growth alive. Sometimes, looking back propels us forward way more than we anticipated.

And, about reframing challenges to learn from them... Ah, this is the gold. It's like suddenly realizing that what seemed like stumbling blocks were actually stepping stones. When we shift our perspective to view setbacks as opportunities for growth, the whole game changes. A nifty question to ask could be, "What's one thing I can learn from this situation?" Suddenly, what seemed like a dead end shows a hidden pathway.

> "It's not failure; it Promoting Well-Being and Satisfaction in Interactions

Ever noticed how a simple question can dramatically shift a conversation? Especially if it's not just any question but one of those *thoughtfully* thrown in queries that show you're genuinely paying attention. I'd go as far as to say that subtle questions... they have this power to coax out responses revealing true feelings. Kinda like, "If you could accomplish one thing today without any barriers, what would it be?" Suddenly, you're no longer just passing the time; you're inviting a peek into someone's aspirations.

"A conversation filled with appreciation is like sunshine to a garden; it spontaneously encourages the blooming of positive emotions."

Imagine a scenario where you focus on appreciation, tossing little verbal bouquets at people's strengths... Yeah, that sounds a bit cheesy when you put it that way. But let's get real for a second. When you talk about what you appreciate in someone's work, or even a small everyday action they did, it does wonders.

Now, hooking into **stories**, those are real gems in conversations. Think back – we all have stories from "back in the day" that shaped us. And when these narratives weave **shared values**, suddenly there's this robust web of understanding knitting us all closer. It makes concepts and ideas tangible. "Remember the time we worked all night to get the project finished?" Suddenly, it's not just work; it's a shared ordeal that values persistence and dedication.

And **active listening**, let's bat an eye at that for a sec. It's like... hanging on to every word, but not for dramatic effect. It's more about giving respect where it's due, facilitating teamwork because you make others feel heard. Who would have thought silence could echo respect, huh?

So, How Do You Make This Work in Real Life?

Let someone finish their sentence, even if you think you know where they're going with it. Basically, keep those ears wide open and your mouth shut—figuratively, an exercise in self-control.

- **Ask for more.** If someone briefly mentions an achievement or effort, don't let it slip. say something like, "I noticed you stayed late yesterday, care to share what you were working on?" Coupons for genuine interest, anyone?
- **Acknowledging emotions but letting them lead the way.** Instead of immediately jumping in to fix problems, a quick acknowledgment goes a long way. "You seem **really** stressed about this deadline. Want to talk out what's on your plate?"

76

- **Using phrases that resonate,** like "Tell me more" or "I see how important this is to you" enhance the depth of a conversation.

Let's drop an informal one—Here's the thing, if you toss in, "I appreciate how you've tackled this," you make someone's day.

"Active listening is not just waiting for your turn to speak; it's about fully engaging with someone's world for that moment."

Stepping back, it's all about keeping it **genuine,** right? These aren't magical formulas but nudges to remodel our daily conversations. Encouraging **open dialogue, stimulating mutual support,** and sincerely appreciating the good stuff in people. And, perhaps, through such exchanges, collectively, we tout toward higher grounds of well-being and satisfaction.

A cheeky side note (just between us): this requires a pinch of bravery. It asks you to shed a layer or two of those defensive sheaths we so love to wear. But guess what? It's **absolutely** worth the hustle. So, next time you're mid-convo, why not throw in a question that matters? Or even better, listen – **really listen.** You'll be surprised by what you find.

Leveraging Strengths through Focused Questions

Sometimes we forget, as individuals, how mighty it is to ask the right questions. When we target our inquiries with precision, magic happens—we begin to unearth abilities and strengths we didn't even know we had. It's like digging through an old chest in the attic and discovering treasures you never knew belonged to you.

Specific questioning allows for strengths discovery. It's a simple thought, right? But let's get real. How often do you finish a day feeling like you could've achieved so much more if only you knew where to direct your energy? A lot, I'd bet. By asking questions designed to drill down into our core competencies and natural talents, we craft this powerful tool for self-discovery. Ask yourself, "What activities fill you with joy and seem to just flow effortlessly?" Or, "When have others praised you for a job well done, and how did that make you feel?"

Identified strengths don't just sit there looking pretty; they **enable pursuit of goals effectively**. You see, once you get a grip on what you actually excel at...Well, it's like finding your personal cheat sheet for life. Exploring goals becomes less about bulldozing through obstacles and more about wisely using your inbuilt competence to breeze through tasks. Like having a natural affinity for numbers might pivot you towards jobs in analytics or accounting.

Regularly emphasizing strengths solidifies confidence. Sounds about right, doesn't it? Imagine giving yourself constant pep talks, highlighting not where you stumbled but where you soared. This process doesn't just sectionalize your ability into good days or bad days but, over time, imbues you with the belief—**the knowledge**—that you inherently have worth and utility. Consider starting a success diary where you jot down small victories facilitated by your strengths. Watching this diary fill up is beyond motivating.

Encouragement inspires colleagues and increases motivation. Leading, whether in small teams or vast organizations, is tremendously influenced by how you deploy questions targeting strengths – both your own and those of your teammates. Offering a colleague honest praise when you notice them excelling builds a support network that feeds positively back into the organizational ethos. Imagine saying, "The way you organized the project schedule played to your strong suit of keeping us on track. We nailed it because of your strategies."

"The essence of strategy is not to outfight everyone but to outthink them."

There's such power in recognizing that. And then, diving a bit further –

"What lies behind us and what lies before us are tiny matters compared to what lies within us."

Absolutely. Harnessing our inner strengths makes pursuits in the external world not just possible, but thrilling.

In practical terms, introduce into your weekly routines small reflection segments. Just a slice of time dedicated to mulling over questions like, "What clicked today and why?" or "What strengths did I tap into to get through a hurdle?". Having a buddy to discuss these with can open up interesting perspectives, too.

So remember, directing those neuron firings in your brain through focused questioning is akin to steering a ship with a competent captain at the helm. The waves might get choppy, the skies might darken, but with your strengths charted out like a map, you're equipped and ready to go. And suddenly, every goal feels just a tad bit closer, and every challenge, well, let's just say, less challenging. As for your toolkit? Those compliment-bolstered questions about what makes you (and those around you) excel, piloting you towards not just being good, but being **exceptionally good** at what you do.

Creating Connections and Building Relationships

Right, let's get into it: creating connections and building relationships isn't just about being nice or professional. It's about digging a bit deeper and finding commonalities that can, well, genuinely make a difference in how we work and interact with each other daily. It's kind of like, with every conversation, you're throwing little anchors of trust and building a strong, interconnected web.

Finding **common ground** is like, "Hey, we're not so different, you and I." It kind of lights up those shared values and goals that might not be apparent right off the bat. When I think about the talks I've had where this clicked, it wasn't about me bombarding someone with expert knowledge or using super fancy terms. It was me being me, and them being them, and both of us realizing, "Wow, we both think this thing is really important."

"The right question at the right time can spark a connection that might have otherwise remained unseen."

One killer way to really get those genuine connections brewing is to ask open questions—these are your golden tickets. They invite honesty and encourage the person you're talking to, to open up. This builds a sense of **trust** that's hard to shake. Plus, it demonstrates that you're actually interested in what they have to say, not just waiting for your turn to speak. It's like saying, "Your thoughts? They matter to me. Let's hear them."

One thing I've learned is, never underestimate the power of **respectful curiosity**. Approaching conversations with a genuine interest and leaving assumptions at the door—turns out, people really respond to that. It sends this signal that says, "I see you as an individual, and I'm genuinely invested in understanding your perspective." It shifts the dynamic in a subtle, yet profoundly positive way.

"To create a space where trust reigns, questions must be the bridges we build—each one paving the way for earnest, open dialogue."

Ah, **emotional understanding**—now that's where it gets interesting. Responding to colleagues' concerns or triumphs with empathy bridges that gap between professional respect and personal rapport. It makes people feel heard and validated, and guess what? They're likely to remember that warmth and return it tenfold. It's this magic formula that not only forges stronger connections but also makes our daily grind a lot more enriching.

Creating connections does take a bit of finesse, yes, but also remember it's mostly about being oneself and nurturing an environment where open questions and empathetic responses are not just encouraged but are part of the very fabric of interaction.

I remember once... Well, let's save that story for another time. But suffice it to say, even the simplest questions have led to some of the most eye-opening conversations for me, ones that have significantly enriched my understanding of those I work with and, honestly, improved our collective work environment hugely.

So, to sum up, a little bit of heart, sprinkled with openness, and driven by genuine curiosity, can be the recipe to transforming our professional sandbox into a treasure chest of connections. And who knows, maybe even lifelong friendships. Just reach out, be authentic, and the rest will follow. It's as simple, and as profoundly impactful, as that.

Strategies for Maintaining a Positive Questioning Approach

In the tangle of everyday challenges, how do we keep the sun shining in our conversations, especially during initial interactions or when the skies seem a bit gray – say, during a pandemic? Positive psychology and systemic inquiry may just be our best allies here. Let's crack into strategies that can keep our dialogues alive.

Firstly, integrating happiness interventions into interviews isn't as complex as it might sound. It could be as simple as beginning with a question that encourages a positive reflection, like, "What's been the best part of your week?" Yeah, it sounds straightforward, but, trust me, the shift in atmosphere it creates is anything but minor.

"A smile is a curve that sets everything straight."

Take this quote to heart. When we implement happiness from the get-go, the vibe changes. We set a precedent: this interaction, no matter how formal, is a space for warmth.

However, the real question is, can we address pressing issues, like the challenges brought about by a pandemic, without veering into doom and gloom? Yes, yes, a thousand times yes. Through intentional communication, we ask about experiences while focusing on resilience and lessons learned, not just hardships faced. For instance, asking, "How have you adapted your routines to stay motivated?" inserts a narrative of overcoming and adapting, a lighter shade on a dark canvas.

Now, to make this approach part of our DNA, repetition is our best friend. Yeah, it might feel a bit robotic at first, trying to incessantly spin things positively, but give it time. This practice isn't about ignoring the negative but about granting equal airtime to the positive. Continuous engagement in this practice ensures it becomes second nature, part of our conversational toolkit.

"The repetition of positive expressions breeds optimism."

Think about including, in your daily interactions, small doses of positivity, like acknowledging a pleasant surprise you encountered or a minor victory you achieved. It doesn't have to be grand; it just has to be positive.

Here's the **nitty-gritty**, the practical side:

- Start every interview with at least one question designed to elicit a positive response.
- When discussions veer towards challenges, intertwine questions focusing on strengths utilized to meet these challenges.

The crux of the matter is, keeping a conversation illuminated with the tinges of positivity does wonders. This isn't just about feeling good; it's about fundamentally transforming the texture of our interactions, making them richer, more productive, and, dare I say, happier.

I've seen it first hand... the shift in people's eyes when they're invited to speak about something that lights them up, even amidst a generally tough topic. It changes the game – not just for the person answering but for the one asking as well, grounding us in a shared human experience that's constructive and, ultimately, uplifting.

Remember, a string of words, however mundane they might seem, carries immense power. The power to **brighten** someone's day, to unearth a forgotten memory of joy, or to plant the seed of a new one. So, why not wield this power intentionally? Let's make every question a small beacon of positivity – after all, we could all use a bit more sunshine in our conversations, couldn't we?

Practical Exercise

Let's *get moving* on an intriguing exercise meant to fuse the cheerful arena of positive psychology with the insightful, expansive view provided by systemic inquiry. Now, what's all this about? Well, stick around, and let's unwrap this little gift together, step by easy step.

Step 1: Identifying what makes you *tick.*First things first, grab a notebook or open a fresh document on your computer. We're about to *get personal.* I want you to jot down things that truly make you happy. Yeah, those moments where you can't help but smile—the genuine, teeth-showing, eye-crinkling smiles. Is it spending time with friends? Reading a good book? Cooking?

Whatever it is, write it down, no judging here.

Step 2: Pinpoint systems at play.

Now, look at that list you've just made... got it? Good. Let's think about this for a second. For each item on your list, identify the systems involved. For example, reading might involve your personal discipline system (finding time), the public library system (getting books), and your mental health system (it relaxes you). Take some time to list these systems beside each happy moment you wrote down.

Step 3: The *juicy* part—connections and intersections.Next, and bear with me, this is where it gets fun; draw lines or make arrows between systems that intersect. Maybe the discipline it takes to cook connects with seeking out new recipes or new cuisines. There's a good chance you'll start seeing connections you haven't noticed before. And if you're like me, sitting there going, "Whoa...," then you're doing it right.

Step 4: Question time.

Ask yourself, "How do these intersecting systems contribute to my happiness?" Try to reflect deeply here, and yes, it's okay if your inner philosopher decides to come out to play. This is where you get those "aha!" moments, so don't skip on the pondering.

Step 5: Bringing in systemic inquiry.

With all these intersections and systems in mind, question how each system affects your ability to experience joy and happiness. Do they support it? Are there any barriers they create? (Trust me, considering barriers is not a downer— it's being smart and proactive).

Step 6: Brainstorming.

This is your chance to think about how you can adjust, shift or connect these systems better to support your happiness. Maybe it's setting a reminder to keep up with your reading, joining a cooking group to enhance that love of cooking—whatever works for you.

Step 7: The plan comes together.

Lastly, sketch out a plan for how you'll implement these changes [Welcome any motivations you discover along the way. Feel free to leave room for spontaneous adjustments as well. Remember, the goal here isn't to fix everything at once— it's to make steps toward a system that better supports your well-being and happiness, bit by bit.

So, there you have it—a slightly cheeky, not-so-serious-but-actually-quite-serious exercise to help you understand how positive psychology and systemic inquiry can blend to improve your life. Give yourself a pat on the back for making it through, and, better yet, give this a try. Who knows what insights and improvements you'll come up with?

Chapter 6: Transformational Leadership and Systemic Questioning

So, here we are, diving headfirst into a topic that, to be honest, gets me all excited — and I hope it does the same for you. Ever heard... well, sure you have... about how certain leaders have this uncanny ability to not just lead but really change the game? Yeah, I'm talking about those folks who seem to see things others don't, and ask the kind of questions that make you think, "Why didn't I think of that?"

These leaders, they've got a knack for something called transformational leadership. It's like they have this magical touch... (I know, I know, nothing magical about hard work and keen insight, but allow me this moment of hyperbole) ...that just brings out the best in their teams. They're the kind that inspires you to do more, be more. But how, you ask? Well, let me tell you, it's about asking the right questions. And not just any questions —I mean those deep, stirring, systemic questions that make you rethink everything.

Oh, and before I forget (which tends to happen when I get into my stories), this isn't just some abstract theory we'll be chattily meandering through. Nope. We're diving into... okay, 'diving' might be a bit ambitious... walking through real stories, insights that tap into our daily lives, if you will. Because, let's face it, who doesn't love a good story?

I bet you're thinking, "Is this going to be another yawn-fest of a chapter that I pretend to read but actually just skim through?" — and to that, I'd say, nope. Promise. We're here to chat, laugh a bit, and maybe — just maybe — have one of those lightbulb moments together. And it all starts with questioning — not just the 'how' and 'what,' but the 'why'... and sometimes the 'why not'.

(Okay, quick personal aside, isn't it fascinating how just asking 'why' can open up a world of understanding? Food for thought.)

Anyway, let's get going. No time like the present to figure out what makes transformational leaders tick and how integrating systematic questioning into our own leadership style could — I'm just gonna say it — change our world. Ready? I thought so. Let's roll.

Inspiring Vision and Purpose with Strategic Questions

When we talk about getting teams to rally around a **vision**—to feel a shared drive and see a unified **purpose**—it largely hangs on the *kind* of questions we throw into the mix. I've found that question trees, those branching sets of inquiries that start from a broad "what if" and stretch out into the specifics, are prime tools for shaping bulletproof mission and vision statements. Now, I say "bulletproof" because, let's face it, in the hustle of reaching targets, it's easy to overlook whether what we're chasing aligns with the bigger picture.

I remember this workshop where we spent an afternoon literally sketching out a question tree on a giant whiteboard... and, yes, it looked as chaotic as it sounds. But by the end of it, everything connected—the messy lines formed a clear path to what we truly aimed to achieve. With every branch, we asked things like, "What truly matters to us?" and "How does this align with what we bring to the table?" It was enlightening.

"What we find changes who we become."

Aligning values is much like finding North on a compass—it guides our decisions, behaviors, and ultimately, keeps us on the right path. A question I always pose for sparking conversation on values alignment is, "In what ways do our personal values reflect in our communal goals?" It's fascinating because it forces a dial-down into the inner mechanics of our motivations, ensuring that our team isn't just working together... but growing together, towards a shared horizon.

Encouraging a space for exploration of what's beyond the present reality is another slice of the vision-casting pie. Forward-looking queries like "Where do we see ourselves in the next five years, and what are steppingstones that can take us there?" opens up the floor to ideas, innovations, and sometimes, to the unexpected roads we might take to our destination. This is where the gold is—the untapped thoughts, the raw potential just lurking beneath the daily operations.

"Questioning is the art of mining our inner potential."

Discussing the **big picture** requires us to step out of the nitty-gritty details and look at the constellation of actions, decisions, and strategies as part of a larger cosmos. Macroscopic questioning reminds us to zoom out... way out. It asks, "How do the pieces fit into the grand scheme of things?" Suddenly, even mundane tasks gain significance because they're no longer just tasks—they're steps in a grand adventure towards something monumental.

A simple exercise I often facilitate involves asking each team member to depict how they see their role in the bigger framework of the organization's vision. Trust me, when people start drawing— yeah, actual drawing—a magical shift happens. They begin to see themselves not just as players, but as creators of that vision, instilling a deeply personal investment in the journey and outcome.

So, how do you craft these dynamic, vision-propelling questions?

- Begin with broad, open-ended questions that invite team members to share their hopes and concerns.
- Narrow down progressively, zooming in on specifics, but maintain the thread that ties it back to the broader vision.
- Always circle back to aligning personal and organizational values—it's what makes the journey meaningful.

Instigating such conversations acts as the catalyst for inspiring a collective vision... and trust me, there's something deeply powerful in seeing a team realize, together, *"Yeah, this is why we do what we do."* It's about connecting the dots, revealing the blueprint of dreams, aspirations, and-plans-yet-to-unfold. And, importantly, it's about recognizing the incredible part every individual plays in painting that bigger picture.

Motivating Teams through Insightful Inquiry

So, you want to learn how to **motivate your team** effectively, using nothing but your words and questions? Yep, I thought you might. See, getting a group of people pumped, focused, and ready to tackle whatever comes their way isn't exactly a walk in the park. But, with the right set of questions? Well, let's just say you can turn that uphill battle into a level playing field.

First up, we're digging into employing solution-focused questions for performance improvement. Now, imagine this... You're sat in a meeting, everyone's throwing around reasons why things aren't moving as fast as they'd like—the classic blame game. Here's where you swoop in, clutch moment, and ask, **"What's one thing we can do right now to make a positive step forward?"**

Kind of changes the whole vibe, doesn't it? That's because you're moving the focus from problem to solution. No more finger-pointing, just pure, constructive brainpower.

Believe it or not, understanding your team's strengths and golden opportunities is as simple as mastering the art of SWOT analysis questions. Chuck in a question like, **"Can anyone share a recent success and what contributed to it?"** Suddenly, you've got a blueprint of your team's superpowers. Follow it up with, **"What can we do to replicate that success in areas we're struggling?"**

and voilà—everyone's seeing the light, not just the looming shadows.

"Hey, what genuinely gets you excited about working on this project?" Notice where I'm going here, bringing engagement into the center stage. By steering the conversation towards personal driving forces, you're basically handing the microphone over to intrinsic motivation—letting it lead the way. When folks open up about what gets their gears turning, that's when the real magic happens: a pathway for sincere engagement reveals itself.

Here's a fun part—**brainstorming creative solutions.** Get the ball rolling with, **"If we could achieve our goal in any way, without any limitations, what out-of-the-box methods would we try?"** This is where you toss mind mapping into the mixer, along with associative questions, turning your brainstorming sessions into powerhouse gatherings of breakthrough ideas.

Speaking of breakthrough ideas...

"The right question at the right moment can spark an island of insights in a sea of uncertainty."

And when seeking those bursts of inspiration...

"Nothing fuels progress more than a room full of minds, igniting each other with question after creative question."

Using colloquial language and creating a cozy chat-like atmosphere makes all the difference. Imagine leaning back in your chair, looking around at your team, and saying, simply, *"What do you think?"*

By stimulating this kind of open dialogue, grounded in insightful inquiry, you're not just another leader. Nope. You're a maestro of motivation, syncing every team member to the rhythm of progress, innovation, and mutual respect.

Remember, folks, tossing around game plans and strategies is fine and all, but if you really want to light that fire of motivation and push your team into a symphony of action, then your golden ticket lies in the power of asking the right, insightful questions... at just the right time.

Driving Change and Innovation with Creative Questions

In the quest for driving change and stimulating innovation within teams or organizations, the use and generation of creative questions plays a pivotal role. Now, speaking from my own experience and some solid practices, I must share how exploring probabilities and possibilities through scenario planning, stimulating a culture of experimentation, questioning assumptions, and the application of design thinking principles can quite literally set the stage for transformative leadership.

First off, creat the blueprints—never underestimate the power of **scenario planning**. It's not just about figuring out what's going to work; it's more about asking, "What if we tried this?" and seeing where that thought can lead. Through imaginative and speculative inquiries, you can spark discussion about numerous future circumstances and their possible impacts. A practical exercise? Gather your team, throw a challenge on the table, and start drumming up as many "what ifs" as you can think about. The aim here is to stretch the imagination to its limits. Sounds fun, right?

"What would happen if we...?"

The aforementioned quote poses the sort of question that encourages people to break out of their comfort zones. That's where innovation begins folks.

Cultivating a **culture of experimentation** requires a baseline of grateful curiosity. This means encouraging questions like, "What's the best that could happen?". In the pursuit to innovate, welcoming failure as part of the process is essential. Because let's face it, it's not just about ticking off the boxes that success brings, but also about learning what doesn't work. When team members feel safe and are acknowledged for their curiosity, the experimentation shift happens quite naturally—an environment where taking calculated risks is not frowned upon.

Now, questioning assumptions—to me, this is a tricky yet necessary one. It's all about shining a light on those hidden biases and blind spots we all carry. It often starts with, "Why have we always done it this way?". These discussed assumptions can sometimes protect outdated methods from being examined and ultimately hinder innovation. It'a about trying not to let them hold us back. You'll find that addressing these questions directly can be both liberating and lead to more comprehensive solutions.

"In what ways might we have been mistaken about...?"

By **applying design thinking principles through an iterative questioning process**, you sort of adopt this diverse mindset that greatly lends itself to innovation. You begin with empathetic questions to genuinely understand the user's experience. After identifying their core needs and issues, you explore, ideate, and prototype through a continuous cycle of improvement.

- Ask: Who are we designing for?
- Identify: What's the problem or need?
- Ideate: What number of different solutions can we come up with?
- Prototype: What's a quick and dirty way to test our ideas?
- Test: How did our user react? How can we improve?

Mixing this approach with a deeply **grateful curiosity** and openness to experimenting, leads to a sprout of insightful and breakthrough solutions—never-say-die spirit for change.

Remember folks, in this quite frankly chaotic process, the key takeaway shouldn't be the sheer volume of questions...but rather, promoting the idea that asking the **right questions at the right time** can be most catalytic. So, my advice? Lean into it! Allow it all: the pauses, shifts, laughter, and yes, even the frustrations—it's all part of the transformative journey. Trust me, been there—done that.

Developing Leaders within Teams through Mentorship

When we're trying to develop leaders within our teams, we really need to keep our eyes on the prize while standing firmly on the ground... maintain high **performance expectations** but keep things real with SMART goals' questions. Yeah, you heard it right, keeping it SMART—Specific, Measurable, Achievable, Relevant, and Time-bound—creates a framework that guides mentees but doesn't strap them down too tightly. It's kinda like saying, "I believe in you, but let's plot this out so it doesn't seem like climbing a mountain every time we set a goal."

Let me throw an example your way to make it clearer: suppose you're mentoring someone keen on improving their public speaking skills. A SMART goal question could look like this, "By next quarter, can you lead at least three meetings and gather feedback to improve on at least two areas identified?" See? Specific, measurable... you get the drift.

Balancing guidance with **autonomy** can be...well, tricky. It's all about finding that sweet spot between directive and non-directive questions. *Think of it as a dance*, where sometimes you lead firmly and other times you let your dance partner take the spotlight. "Where do you see yourself leading in this project?" versus "I think you should take the lead on this project because X, Y, Z..." It's a subtle art.

Active listening and asking **open-ended, exploratory questions** just can't be overlooked. It's like opening a door instead of a window —you're inviting an avalanche of perspective instead of a gentle breeze. Questions like, "What's your take on our current strategy?" or "How would you approach this challenge?" invite deeper thought and engagement. And it works because being heard feels...pretty **phenomenal**, doesn't it?

Oh, and let's not forget about encouraging reflective practice. Now, that's where the gold is. Getting your mentees in the habit of **self-assessment** and laying out their *future bright spots* are like giving them a map and a torch in the world of leadership. A question like, "Looking back, what could have gone better in your presentation, and how?" supports this beautifully.

"Action is the foundational key to all success."

This quote hits the bullseye. It's all about action — doing, failing, learning, redoing, and eventually shining. By asking the right kinds of questions during mentorship, we're basically arming our future leaders with the ability and confidence to carve their paths towards success diligently.

To bundle this up, it's essential not to underestimate the power of boldly moving forward with an authentic self-assessment to set goals:

"The quality of your life is determined by the quality of questions you ask yourself."

It underscores, yet again, the importance of introspection and constant growth, not only in leadership but in everyday aspects of life too.

In essence, mentoring is a critical component of leadership development that balances on the tightrope of nurturing and empowering. So, roll up your sleeves, get involved with your team, and let the magic of mentorship unfold in real-time. It's all about making those connections, growing together, and of course, asking the **smart, systemic questions** at the right times. Trust me, the transformation this brings to your team will not just be remarkable — it'll be downright inspiring.

Crafting a Legacy of Leadership through Reflective Questions

So, you're on this path, trying to be **better** at what you do, right? And may I say, steering through the *world of leadership* is no small feat. It requires not just honing your skills but also continuously questioning the ground you stand on. It's about asking what went well and...what could go **even better** of?

Let's kick off with **continuous learning**. Life's all about learning, ain't it? When you hit a success, pause. Instead of just patting yourself on the back, pull out the magnifying glass and examine— what made it work? Was it the teamwork, your planning, or maybe a mix? Here's the deal—you keep doing what worked, but, there's a twist. Ask yourself, "What could make it **even better** next time?" Suddenly, you're not just resting on your laurels but **building** a staircase to new heights.

Now, leaning in toward **empathy**. A word massively thrown around, but how do we embed it into our leadership style? Meet *appreciative inquiry*. It's like you're mining for gold in people's experiences and views... but with a map. It's about seeing the glass half full, not to ignore problems, but to **build on** that's already solid. And **humble inquiry?** Well, that requires mastering the art of asking questions that invite, not intimidate. "Tell me more about how you reached this solution" instead of "Why did you do it this way?"... see the difference?

Moving on...to assess **organizational impact**, try using impact evaluation frameworks. Sounds fancy, but in essence, you're painting a picture of your organization's footprint. It's not just about profits, though. It's about how you—together with your team—shape the environment around you. **Did we leave it better than we found it?** And how can we **maintain** that journey towards progress? Sometimes, the image comes out less vibrant than you hoped, but guess what? That's your **catalyst** for change.

"Leadership is learning from the past, envisioning the future, and acting in the present."

Speaking of moving forward, let's talk about climbing this **mountain called career** with...you guessed it, career development questionnaires. It's not an exam, don't worry. It's more like a map for your hike up leadership mountain. Where are you now? Where do you want to be? Despite the simplicity, these questions have the power to bring revelations to your *leadership journey*.

So, take on this recipe for **building a leadership legacy**:

- **Reflect** on what went well,
- **Aim** higher by questioning how to make it even better,
- **Foster empathy** by appreciating strengths and encouraging honest conversations,
- Use **frameworks** to gauge the impact like a pro,
- And always, **map out your career with quesitonaries tailored to guide your growth.**

"Reflection is the lamp of the heart. If it departs, the heart will have no light."

By now, you might think, all this talking, does it really work? Well, the proof is in the **pudding** (or in this case, the leadership). Reflective questions don't just shape leaders; they shape individuals ready to face challenges with a toolkit full of **resilience**, empathy, and foresight. And **guess what?** You're building that toolkit **right now**. Keep sharpening those tools, keep asking the right questions, and watch as your legacy unfolds...one inquiry at a time.

Practical Exercise

Alright, folks - we're going to dive headfirst (not in a literal sense, mind you) into a pretty neat exercise based around **Chapter 6: Transformational Leadership and Systemic Questioning**. So, what's this all about, then? Well, let me give you a runaround before we get all up in the details.

What's the Big Idea?

Our goal is pretty simple yet incredibly vital - we're looking to get our hands dirty with the whole concept of **transformational leadership**; think of it as leading in a way that not only encourages good vibes and forward-thinking in a group but also stirs up a positive change. And that includes getting up close and personal with **systemic questioning**. It's like trying to see the bigger picture by asking smarter, not harder, questions.

Step-by-Step - Let's Break It Down

1. Background Chat

First things first, we're going to set the stage. I want you to think of a leader you personally admire - anyone from a favorite teacher to a community leader or even a boss that had your back. Jot down what makes them stand out to you. Is it the way they talk, make decisions, or perhaps how they motivate their team?

2. Enter Transformational Leadership

Next, taking the traits you've just scribbled down, I want you to match them against what we know transformational leaders do. Do they *inspire, challenge the norm, foster an environment of creativity,* or *care for the individual's growth*? Draw a couple of lines connecting the dots. Starting to see any patterns here?

3. Time for a Quiz!

Okay, not a_dreaded_ quiz but a cool, reflexive one. Answer these - "Which quality of a transformational leader do I see in myself?" and "Which area could use a bit of work?" Be honest; it's just for you.

4. Pop Quiz Hotshot

Remember systemic questioning we kinda hovered around earlier? Well, here's the gist - it's all about asking **the right questions** that get you thinking about things in a holistic way. So, here comes your task: think of a problem or a project bubbling up at school, work, or home. Now, craft three wicked-smart questions that force you to consider the project from a totally different angle.

For example:

- "What's the underlying need behind this project?"
- "Who are all the people affected by it, and how does it impact them?"
- "What long-term effects could this have, both good and bad?"

5. Reflect and Share (if you're feelin' brave)

Sit back and take a hot minute to pour over everything you've jotted down. You starting to feel these concepts clicking into place? If you're feeling extra brave, why not share your findings or reflections with a friend, mentor, or heck, even throw them out in a group discussion? Sometimes, vocalizing our thoughts brings new insights.

And who knows – maybe through this exercise, we might just nod to each other, realizing, "Ah, so *this* is what transformational leadership is all about." Plus, maybe you've discovered some cool things about yourself as a leader or an inquirer. Maybe the systemic questions have opened up a new way for you to tackle problems from all angles?

Well, friends – you made it through! I've got to say, you've got a knack for handling this stuff with style and curiosity. Keep asking those big questions and eyeing those inspiring traits in leaders all around you. Who knows, someone might be jotting down notes about *your* leadership style soon.

Chapter 7: Applying Systemic Questions in Various Contexts

Ever wandered what makes a conversation really 'click'? Why in some chats, you're left scratching your head - while in others, you feel like you've really gotten to the heart of things? It's like there's this secret sauce, and wouldn't it be great if we could all get a taste? Well, that's what we're here to talk about in this part of the book— getting to the gist with systemic questions in a plethora of situations.

I mean, it's not rocket science, but it does call for a bit of finescing - and, alright, a bit of psychology too. It's all about understanding the person on the other end of the conversation, really getting into their shoes. (Personal confession: I used to be terrible at this...thought I knew it all. Spoiler alert—I didn't.)

So, why focus on systemic questions, you ask? Simple. They're, like, the Swiss Army knife of communications. Being able to toss the right question at the right time, in the right context, it's...pretty cool. And trust me, it's not just useful for therapists or folks in suits sitting in boardrooms. Whether it's smoothing over dinner debates, acing job interviews, or just trying to connect better with your moody teenager — these techniques can be a game changer.

And yeah, let's be honest here, this isn't about mastering some manipulative tricks to control conversations. It's...deeper than that. It's about enriching connections, finding clarity, maybe even helping someone (or yourself) through a rough patch.

In this chapter, we'll walk through various everyday scenarios - from the pesky professional pickle to those awkward social spa-outs where you wish the ground would just swallow you up. I'll share anecdotes, maybe spill a bit about my own faux pas along the way, and we'll look at why certain questions just... work.

So grab your metaphorical snorkel — we're going dipping into the riveting world of systemic questions. (And if you're not ready try this in your life, no sweat. At least you'll have some cool party talk, right?)

Adaptation of Questions in Personal Relationships

When we talk about personal relationships, we're venturing into a space that's both delicate and dynamic. The true art lies in asking the right kind of questions... Yes, **circular questioning**, **understanding perspectives**, **utilizing open-ended questions**, and **developing self-awareness** through systemic thinking- these are our tools.

So, let's break it down. Relational dynamics—sounds complicated, doesn't it? But here's a thought—what if, instead of playing detective, we play guide? Picture this: using circular questioning not to corner anyone... but rather to initiate a shared exploration. It's about creating a loop of **inquiry and insight** where each question and its response opens up a new layer of understanding. To me, circular questioning feels like dancing together, where each step uncovers more about the other person's rhythm.

Understanding individual perspectives in relationships... now that's a game-changer. Let's get real, we all see our world in specific ways due to our unique experiences. Recognizing this can shift the dynamic. Instead of seeing a reaction as "difficult" or "obstinate," asking the right question can peel back layers, revealing **hidden beliefs and emotions**. And what are the right questions? Open-ended ones. "How did you feel when that happened?" or "What do you believe about...?" These kind of inquiries can throw the doors wide open to what a person truly believes and feels.

"Questions are the breath of life to a conversation."

Here's something personal: when I started integrating systemic thinking exercises into my own life, it was a game-changer. Systemic thinking practically forces you to become self-aware. It encourages digging deep, questioning not just the world around you but the world within you. And in relationships, this introspection, powered by questions, can **bridge gaps** we didn't even know existed.

Utilizing open-ended questions during conversation is like handing someone the paintbrush to draw their **inner landscape**. And, here comes the interesting part—guess what happens when you show genuine interest in their painting? They're more likely to ask about yours. This reciprocity is the fundamental **core** of developing connections.

"Self-awareness is the canvas of our interpersonal relationships."

Let me share a quick exercise that I found transformationally helpful:

1. Jot down three open-ended questions you could ask someone in a personal relationship. Think broad, no yes/no queries.
2. Narcissists next, write how you might feel answering those same questions.
3. Try these questions in an actual conversation but be genuinely curious about the answers.

Here's the kicker - questions, especially the systemic ones we're talking about, aren't just tools for understanding others; they're a pathway to **understanding ourselves**.

Remember (sorry for using this word—old habits die hard!), words are powerful, questions even more so. Driving at the heart of what makes us *us*, and having the courage to ask those thoughtful, reflective questions can utterly **alter the landscape of personal**

relationships. So the next time you're pondering on how to improve your connection with someone... maybe, just maybe, the answer lies in not just talking, but asking.

Tailoring Questions for Professional Development

When we explore the world of professional development, it's all about pushing the boundaries, isn't it? I mean, we're constantly hunting for ways to better understand our strengths and weaknesses, not to mention how our usual patterns of behavior play a role in our overall work performance. Let's not forget, we're also on a mission to foster a growth mindset by teasing out new perspectives and strategies.

So, where do systemic questions come into play in all this? Well, **integrating systemic thinking** into leadership development programs isn't just fancy talk. It's about cutting through the surface to get to the heart of how we operate within our professional settings. Picture this: you're in a leadership role, and you start noticing some recurring issues within the team. Instead of just reacting on the spot, what if you stepped back and asked, "What patterns can I identify here, and how might they be influencing the bigger picture?"

"What existing strengths can we lean on that we haven's fully recognized until now?" Now that's a question that shifts the focus, isn't it? Suddenly, you're not zeroing in on problems. You're hunting for hidden treasures within your team's skill set.

And how about behavior patterns affecting work performance? Consider asking, "In what situations do our reactions contribute to this outcome, and how could we respond differently next time?" This line of inquiry opens a whole new can of worms... in a good way, of course!

Encouraging a growth mindset is another cornerstone. Questions like, "What's a recent challenge we faced, and how did our perception of it influence the outcome?" can be game-changing. It nudges people to reconsider not just what happened, but how their framing of the event shaped their experience.

The real kicker, though, is when we start looking at **reframing strategies**. Ever thought about asking, "If we considered this not as a setback, but as a stepping stone, how does the solution change?" Boom! That question alone can transform the proverbial "dead-end" into an "opportunity to innovate." It's all about that mindset shift.

Integrating systemic thinking into leadership realms doesn't need to be a giant leap. Sometimes, it's the smaller steps, the targeted questions that lead to profound shifts. Imagining weaving this kind of questioning into everyday interactions... It changes the game, making every conversation an opportunity for reflection and growth.

"Asking the right questions at the right time isn't about getting answers. It's about stimulating curiosity, opening doors."
"It's not just about addressing the issues at hand, but understanding their roots and interconnections in the broader system."

Personal tales from the trenches have taught me that this stuff works. There was a time when simply by shifting the questions we asked during review sessions, the whole team started to **identify its own growth opportunities**. Instead of me pointing out areas for improvement, they were bringing insights to the table, keen on exploring new solutions—and all because the questions encouraged reflection and self-assessment.

Now, imagine applying this mindset to your leadership development program. Start with the self, leading by example:

- Regularly reflect on your own responses and behaviors.
- Practice asking yourself systemic questions.

- Begin integrating these questions into your interactions with the team.

Bit by bit, this approach can redefine professional growth, making it a journey of collective insight rather than solitary introspection. The beauty of it all? It starts with a simple question. So, what's stopping us from asking?

Enhancing Team Dynamics with Specific Inquiries

We all know teams can be, well, complicated, right? In every group or organization, there's always a mix of personalities, working styles, and, frankly, the inevitable clashes that come with trying to get things done together. But, through all that, there's something almost magical about the way asking the right questions, at the right time, can clarify so much—or even solve problems before they really get going.

For starters, let's think about the *art of examining team dynamics.* It's about stopping and really looking at how people interact—who talks the most, who sits back a bit more, and (yes) even who rolls their eyes whenever a certain project is mentioned. It sounds like snooping, but it's more like being a super attentive friend. I once observed, during regular team meetings, that one team member always offered ideas, which somehow were never acknowledged, let alone discussed. When I asked the team, "What if we give everyone a minute to share their thoughts on this, without interruptions?" it wasn't long before these overlooked ideas started reshaping our project for the better.

Identifying conflicts? Yeah, I've had my fair share of walking into those. But, through a cascade of carefully considered questions like, "Can you help me understand what specifically you're concerned about here?" it's possible to dig beneath the surface. Often, it's not the immediate issue that's the real problem—it's something several steps before that, something that was never addressed.

To walk the talk of stimulating individual participation and collaboration, I lean heavily on questions tailored to pull people out of their shells while pushing the team to debrief together. In a way, it's a bit like constructing a bridge while you're already halfway across it. For example, asking, "What's one idea you've been sitting on, unsure if it's right for this project?" immediately invites inclusion and demonstrates the value each person brings to the table.

And we cannot, I repeat, cannot, overestimate the importance of *developing empathy* amongst team members. One technique I adore is the 'future backward' question. This involves asking, "Looking back from a successful future, what might we have dismissed as a small detail that actually made a big difference?" Encouraging empathy through **systemic questioning** such as...

"Imagine yourself in their shoes—what would be frightening about bringing your idea forward?"

...literally puts us in a position to appreciate our team members in a dimension we might not have considered before.

Why do these specific inquiries work? Well, it's because they go beyond the superficial. Consider the emphasis on...

"Why is this important to you?"

...this simple question propels understanding and real, meaningful conversations layered with personal insights.

My journey through applying systemic questioning in team dynamics has shown me, time and again, that by genuinely including **everyone's perspectives and encouraging deep, empathetic connections,,** we're not just solving today's challenges—we're preemptively softening tomorrow's pitches and falls. And, maybe more importantly, we're building a team that's got the sort of positive vibes where everyone wants to pitch in, try harder, and sincerely celebrate each setback transformed into a success story.

Systemic Questions in Conflict Resolution

Ever been caught in a the sticky web of conflict, wondering, "Okay, where do we even begin to sort this mess out?" Well, you're not alone. It's tricky, figuring out how to get two heads—or sometimes more—to nod in agreement, especially when they've been locking horns over something. But I've got a little secret weapon for you: **systemic questions**.

Take root causes, for example. More often than not, what's bubbling on the surface isn't the whole picture. I like to use something called *circular questioning*. It's like playing detective, going around in circles, but the good kind. You start asking, "What led up to this?", peeling back layers until—voila—you hit the core issue. It's like finding that one loose thread that, once pulled, helps everything else come undone, easy and smooth.

Now, for looking at disputes, here's a nugget of truth:

"There are always at least two truths in any conflict, each believed to be the only one."

We've gotta hammer it home. Exploring **alternative perspectives** is super clutch. It's...

...like stepping into someone else's shoes. Only when we try on those shoes, perhaps uncomfortably snug or a tad too roomy, do we have this "ah-ha" moment, realizing, "Okay, maybe they've got a point."

One thing I swear by is pushing for an open dialogue. It's critical to keep the channels clear, letting all the muck flow out freely so fresh thoughts can flow in. Listen, if the people involved don't feel like they're heard, It's like yammering away to a brick wall—frustrating and futile. Encouraging folks to really talk, and not just wait for their turn to splurge out what's in their mind, could **change the whole game**.

Negotiation—now, that's a whole ballet by itself. But who said you need to ace in ballet to make wonderful moves? Using systemic inquiry is much like inviting someone to a dance, where each question leads subtly to another. It's about keeping a beat. Simple cues like, "What outcome would meet your needs here?", can really open up the floodgates.

Weaving through conflict with questions isn't a walk in the park, but it's definitely a hike worth taking. Let me lay it out bullet point-style for nice appetizer bites:

- Use **circular questioning** to drill down to (not so) mysterious roots of the conflict.
- Give everyone a stage to strut their perspective— it enriches the plot!
- **Open dialogue**: work it till the mic's all warm and fuzzy.
- Negotiation is your tango. Lead gracefully.

Ever had those moments where, mid-conflict, you think to yourself, "Why can't we all just get along?" Here's another gem:

"Asking the right question might just be the answer."

By injecting systemic questions into heart of the dispute, voila, you'd be surprised how dilemmas start to resemble dialogues rather than trials. Let's warm up to the idea. Why? Because stepping away from stereotypes, listening in 4K detail, and sharing the stage can turn clashing swords into hope-filled olive branches.

Bottom line? It's not always about sidestepping puddles but learning how to gasp, splash, and laugh, even in the thick muddy ones. Conflicts? Chaotic, maybe—a lost cause, never. So go ahead, ask away. Maybe, just maybe, you'll find the keys to short of a neat car.

Customizing Questions for Different Audiences

When we start digging into the **art of questioning,** it quickly becomes clear that there's no one-size-fits-all approach. And that's okay. Actually, scratch that—it's more than okay. It's necessary. Why, you ask? Well, consider this: The way we phrase questions can either open up a conversation or shut it down faster than you can say, "Oops, my bad."

Adapting systemic questioning techniques based on cultural backgrounds is like trying to select the perfect gift for someone. You want to make sure it fits, feels right, and, most importantly, is appreciated. So, take a moment and think... (Yes, right now!) Have you ever found yourself in a situation where a question, perfectly normal in your culture, raised eyebrows in another? Been there, done that. A powerful reminder: context matters—a lot.

"What might seem curious in your culture could be considered intrusive in another. Respect is key."

Let's jump to tailoring circular questioning according to age groups. Ah, this one's fun and challenging, all wrapped in one. Here's the thing—**kids** aren't just smaller versions of us. They see the world through a kaleidoscope of possibilities; every question can lead to a quest full of wonder. Asking them what they imagine rather than expect paves the way for creativity. For **teenagers,** ensure your questions acknowledge their growing independence; grant them the dignity of their process. As for **adults**? Include them in the circle by seeking their insights on how they've seen situations evolve over time. This fosters a connected and reflective space for conversation.

"Circles have no beginning or end, much like the questions that guide us to deeper understanding and connections."

Getting a bit more personal, let's talk about addressing diverse needs within family systems. Think of your family gatherings... yeah, I see that smile. Diverse perspectives around the same table can be enriching yet challenging. Crafting conversations that consider everyone's voice—without stepping on grandma's toes or making the teenager roll their eyes—is an art in itself. Start with questions that invite each person to contribute from their vantage point, valuing everyone's unique place in the family tapestry.

Alright, how do we weave systemic thinking into educational settings, you ask? Imagine transforming the classroom into an ecosystem where curiosity thrives, and mistakes are merely stepping stones. Instead of merely focusing on the 'right' answers, encourage questions that explore the 'how' and 'why', turning the tables and allowing students to become the questioners. This shift not só promotes critical thinking but also nurtures a sense of ownership and engagement among students.

Practical exercise time: Why not script your next conversation? Whether it's planning to converse with someone from a different cultural background or organizing a family meeting, jot down a couple of questions ahead of time. Make sure they're open, respectful, and genuinely curious. Then, observe. You might be surprised at how the dialogue unfolds, leading to more insightful and meaningful exchanges.

Okay, I kind of went on a bit of a tangent there, but hopefully, it sparked some curiosity in you. Adapting your questioning technique isn't just about modifying the words; it's about shifting the mindset, promoting empathy, respect, and genuine curiosity towards the perspectives of others. So, next time you're gearing up for a conversation, pause... Are you asking the right questions for your audience?

Achieving Desired Outcomes Through Focused Inquiry

Knowing the **right questions** can make all the difference. Like how you talk to a friend who's had a rough day. You don't just throw advice their way, right? Similarly, when facing *complex issues*, understanding comes from asking questions—really good ones.

Applying conceptualization techniques is all about getting a bird's eye view. Think of it as trying to solve a puzzle, but first, you need to see the big picture. Once that's clear, it gets easier to see how everything fits together. Break down problems into bite-sized pieces, and suddenly, they don't look so intimidating.

Let's talk about reframing strategies. Ever find yourself thinking, "I can't do this" or "It won't work"? That's where reframing jumps in to challenge those limiting beliefs. With a slight tweak in perspective, what seemed like a dead end—might not be, like seeing a detour as a scenic route instead of an annoyance.

"The mind once stretched by a new idea, never returns to its original dimensions."

Circular questioning has this magical way of developing self-understanding. It's not just about understanding yourself in isolation but how you fit into the larger picture. It's like when you reflect on your actions within a group. Things start lighting up, contributing to personal and collective growth.

Integrating systemic therapy insights into other therapy models such as psychodynamic, family, and group therapies, opens up new pathways. It creates a richer, fuller approach to understanding human behavior in its social context. By comparing notes between methods, practitioners can pull from a broader toolkit to help their clients better.

But, you know, sometimes we underestimate the **power of questions**. Here's another saying that sticks:

"Ask the right questions if you're going to find the right answers."

When applying systemic questions across different contexts, there's a rhythm to it... It's more **art than science**. You've got to feel out the moment, understand the flow of the conversation, and know when to interject with that thought-provoking question.

So, how can anyone, not just therapists or leaders, use these inquiries to improve interactions and outcomes?

- First, **actively listen**. I mean really listen, not just wait for your turn to speak.
- Reflect back on what's being said. This shows you're engrossed in the conversation.
- Tailor your questions. Adapt them to fit the situation and the people involved. No one-size-fits-all here.

A fun little exercise I sometimes recommend involves something I like to call "question brainstorms." If there's an issue at hand, take about [*insert reasonable yet inappropriate*] minutes to jot down all the questions that come to mind about it. Don't worry if they seem silly; this is your creative process stirring.

By integrating these strategies—from framing your questions rightly, challenging beliefs, to incorporating systemic insights into broader therapeutic practices—you craft a solid groundwork for understanding and action. So, the next time you are caught in the whirlwind of life's complexities, step back...think... What question haven't I asked yet? That might just be the key to unlocking a new pathway forward.

Practical Exercise

Alright folks, we're gonna explore something super interesting. We'll focus on applying **systemic questions** in various exciting contexts. Now, don't fret, this isn't going to be one of those yawn-inducing, stare-at-the-clock kinds of exercises. Instead, it's pretty much about unraveling the **magic** that happens when we ask the right questions at the right time. Ready to roll up your sleeves? Let's get started!

First thing's first: what in the world are **systemic questions,** you might ask. Well, think of them as the Swiss Army knife in the conversational world. They're a way to open up discussions, get people thinking, and, most importantly, they can shift perspectives quicker than a rabbit... doing something very quick. So, hang tight as we explore how you can make the most out of them.

Step 1: *Finding the right setting* - Picture a situation or context where dialogue feels a bit like walking through mud. Got it? Now, that's where you're going to try this out. It could be anything from a group project that's going nowhere fast because no one agrees on anything, or a family dinner where the air is so thick with tension, you could cut it with a knife.

Step2: *Craft your toolkit* - Before you jump into the fray, think about what you want to achieve with your questions. Are you trying to soothe tensions, encourage a different way of seeing things, or simply gather as much information as possible? Write down your goal. Yeah, literally, jot it down somewhere because—believe it or not—seeing your mission in black and white can be a pretty powerful motivator.

Step 3: *Generating your systemic questions* - This is the fun part. Plan to ask questions that highlight relationships, differences, and changes over time instead of pointing fingers. Instead of something accusatory like, "Why are you always so negative?" how about, "In what ways have you seen us succeed as a team despite challenges?" See the twist? It's all about focusing on the positive, not the trapdoors and problems.

113

Step 4: *Engage stealth mode (or just be subtle)* - Now, armed with your questions, enter your chosen setting. But here's the catch: don't just throw your questions out like confetti. Be smooth. Weave them into the existing conversation. Pay close attention, listen actively, and when the moment feels right—**bam!** Drop your systemic question gently into the mix and watch as the atmosphere begins to shift.

Step 5: *Reflection zone*- After implementing your brilliantly crafted questions, make some time to reflect on how they were received. Did the conversation flow change? Did people seem more open to sharing and listening? This isn't just patting yourself on the back time, though it's also important (who doesn't like feeling like a conversation wizard?). Reflecting helps you get better at this with each attempt.

To wrap this wild ride up (and kudos for sticking around till the end), treat each application of systemic questions like a personal experiment. Some will go astonishingly well, others might fall flat— and that's all part of the learning curve. Plus, conversations, like humans, can be peculiar beasts. What works wonders in one scenario may not even turn a head in another. That's cool, really.

It's all about fine-tuning your questions muscles and growing a bit each time you give it a shot. Keep at it, write down a few reflections, adjust your questions accordingly, and watch yourself slowly but surely become a **master of the art**. Trust me, it's a priceless skill to have up your sleeve.

Chapter 8: Mastering the Craft of Systemic Questioning

So, I've been thinking... mastering the craft of systemic questioning isn't just about firing off questions left, right, and center—nope. It's more like becoming a detective in your own right, where every question leads you closer to the heart of the mystery, which in this case, are the deeper, more profound understandings of pretty much any topic under the sun. Now, why is this skill so darn important, you ask? Well, think about the last time you got really curious— like, childhood-level curious—about something. That energy, that drive to get to the bottom of things, is what we're aiming to channel here.

I'm gonna be honest with you, perfecting this requires a hefty dose of reflection ("Am I really listening, or just waiting to speak?" hits hard, doesn't it?), and a fair bit of finesse to pull off in real-life conversations without sounding like you're interrogating your pal, Greg, over coffee on a Tuesday morning. Through this chapter, I'm going to share anecdotes, maybe throw in a clumsy attempt or two at humor—just to keep things lively—and of course, give you practical tips.

Seriously, think about how empowered you feel when you finally understand something complex after breaking it down piece by piece? That's the magic I want us to capture together. By the end, I imagine us perched on the edge of our seats, craving to apply systemic questioning in every corner of our lives, from the mundane to the monumental (without annoying everyone around us into silence, ideally). So, are you in? Because, really, it's not just about asking better questions... it's about building connections that get you closer to the reality you're curious about, while inviting others along for the ride. And let's be real, wouldn't it be cool to be that friend—

the detective friend who always gets to the bottom of things? Yes, I thought so too.

Continuous Learning and Improvement in Questioning Techniques

Mastering the craft of questioning isn't just about knowing which question to ask... it's about the **constant grind**—yeah, I said grind, because let's be honest, that's what it feels like sometimes—of refining and adapting your technique. Think of it like perfecting a recipe; you gotta tweak it, taste it, and sometimes, start from scratch with a different spice. The same goes for questioning; the magic ingredient often... is reflection.

Reflecting on past questions and the answers they elicited is like looking in a mirror that shows you not just your face but your mind. It's about asking yourself, "Did my question open up a new door or did it hit a wall?" Every. Single. Question. It's a stepping stone to a better one next time. It reminds me of this gem:

"The quality of your questions determines the richness of your answers."

And let's not forget the powerhouse of inspiration sitting right next to us—or in our vast internet realm, which is free for the taking for anyone willing. Observing how the big guns, the skilled questioners, weave their tapestry of dialogue with finesse is like getting a front row seat at a masterclass for free! Seeing their technique, how they lay down their questions with such precision... it's enlightening, and honestly, a bit intimidating, but in a good way. It bulldozes a path in your mind for you to try replicating—or better yet—adapting their technique with your personal flair. Because, let's face it, imitation might be flattery, but originality? That's game.

Practicing regularly with different folks and topics... now, that's where things get really spicy. You ever talk about quantum physics with a musician or break down Beethoven's 5th with a physicist? It's not just an exercise in patience, but a pathway to incredible versatility in your questioning skills. Testing your pitches across different fields throws you curveballs you didn't even know were part of the game.

And feedback—sweet, sometimes bitter, feedback—is the cherry on top. Asking for, and yes, implementing, feedback makes our questioning muscles flex and grow. People will point out blind spots you didn't know were there, like:

"I didn't quite catch your drift, could you reword that?"

And boom, you have a tangible lead on how to adjust your questioning compass.

So, here are the **checks and balances** on perfecting your craft:

- Reflect on each question and its journey—**the introspection portion**.
- Observe and analyze the masters—call that **the inspired Fan Club phase**.
- Practice, practice, practice—with a heterogenous mix, considering it **the fieldwork phase**.
- Feedback's the one you love but also fear—**think of it as face-mirror moment**, right?

Remembering that no matter how smooth or rough the road gets, each setback or leap forward is shoring up your foundation in this dynamic skill set. Like piecing together a complex jigsaw puzzle, the full picture of your progress might only reveal itself over time. So keep prodding, exploring, and questioning—not just others, but yourself too. The art of asking powerhouse questions lies in the journey... not just the destination.

The Journey of Becoming a Skilled Inquirer

So, you want to master the craft of systemic questioning, huh? Well, it's one rollercoaster of a ride, filled with ups and downs, twists and turns, and a side of questioning everything you thought you knew about communication... Sounds fun, doesn't it? Let's just say, it's not for the faint of heart—but, if you're anything like me, you know that the best things in life are often those that challenge us the most.

First things first: this field requires a **commitment** to consistently practice your questioning techniques. Imagine practicing guitar; you wouldn't expect to be playing like Santana after a few weeks, right? It's the same with learning to craft questions that open doors and minds.

And where do we find inspiration and guidance? Through **learning from mentors, peers, and literature** on masterful questioners. It's a bit like having a map when you're lost in the woods; these resources guide you, providing insights and illuminating the path ahead.

Now... patience. I know, I know, we live in a world where everything is needed yesterday, but **cultivating patience** and a willingness to learn and grow over time is key.

As for **welcoming challenges** encountered during this learning process... well, let's just say it builds character. You're going to ask questions that fall flat, misread the room, or even challenge someone accidentally. It's all part of the learning curve.

"Great questioning is an art that is molded through practice, reflection, and more practice. Each interaction is a brushstroke on the canvas of our conversational masterpiece."

Leaning on mentors and literature can really make a difference, providing that lightbulb moment when you least expect it. Ever read a line in a book and think, "Wow, this speaks to me"? It happens, and it's golden when it does.

And what about patience? Oh, this takes time—lots of it. Seeing the fruits of your labor doesn't happen overnight. It's about playing the long game, celebrating the small wins, and keeping your eye on the prize.

"(What if I fail?) Good question. Remember, each misstep is a learning opportunity, guiding us toward becoming adept in the art of asking."

And before you know it, you'll notice changes. That sense of **don't know what you don't know** starts to fade, and bit by bit, you'll develop a knack for asking just the right question at just the right moment.

Here are some practical steps to guide you along the way:

- **Practice, practice, practice.** Take every chance you get to ask questions, even outside of professional settings.
- **Seek feedback.** After conversations, reflect on what went well and what could be better. Ask a trusted friend or mentor for their honest opinion.
- **Explore literature and videos** on the topics of effective communication and transformational leadership. There's a well of knowledge out there waiting for you.
- **Observe master questioners.** Pay attention to their timing, their tone, and how they phrase their questions to elicit deep responses.

And through it all, remember, every master was once a beginner. It's okay to feel lost, confused, or frustrated. These feelings are simply signposts letting you know you're on the right path... the path to becoming a skilled inquirer.

So, keep pushing forward, keep asking, and—who knows?—one day, someone might be looking up to you as their mentor, facing the delightful complexities of systemic questioning.

Building a Repertoire of Powerful Questions

When you're trying to master the art of systemic questioning... well, it's kinda like learning a new language. At first, it's all about memorizing useful phrases and understanding the grammar—that is, developing questions tailored to a variety of contexts and individuals. Then, you start dabbling in more advanced questioning techniques, like that fancy thing called precision questioning. Trust me, integrating thoughtfully selected questions into conversations can almost feel... magical.

Every conversation is an opportunity to practice, observe, and learn. Ever noticed how a well-placed question can shift the entire direction of a dialogue? It's like those moments in movies where everything changes with a single line. Pretty powerful stuff.

Take precision questioning, for instance. This isn't just about asking more questions. It's about asking the **right questions**. Imagine you're peeling an onion. You're getting closer to the heart of what someone's really saying or feeling with each layer—you just have to know which leaves to peel.

Incorporating these into our conversations requires a knack for timing and context. It's not simply, "Hey, let me throw in this awesome question I learned," but more, "Is this the right moment for this question? Will it add value, or could it confuse things?"

And here's where the magic truly happens; reflecting on the impact these questions have on our conversations:

"It is not the answer that illuminates, but the question."

Powerful, right? A question can illuminate thoughts and ideas that were lurking just beneath the surface, ready to be unmeshed by, you guessed it, another question.

Now, for a bit of narrative on this. Imagine you're sitting at a table with colleagues or friends. The discussion is decent, but nothing earth-shattering... until you drop in that precision ducted question. Suddenly, the conversation takes a different turn, diving deeper than before, unearthing insights or opinions that were hidden until that very moment. That's the prowess you wield with systemic questioning.

Here's another gem to appreciate:

"Ask the hard questions, and the soft answers will follow."

But how do you get there? Here are a few steps to consider:

- Listen actively. Every spoken word might carry the seed of a follow-up question.
- Practice empathy. Understanding others' perspectives can reveal the questions you need to ask.
- Know your goals. Align your questions with what you wish to achieve in the dialogue.

A moment of personal reflection from my side (since, well, who doesn't love a good aside?): I've found that keeping a journal of impactful questions and answers from my daily conversations has been surprisingly enlightening. It's one thing to theorize about systemic questioning; it's another to see its effects play out in your own interactions.

Remember, learning to ask the right question at the right time is a skill that takes practice, patience, and a bit of bravery, too. Why bravery? Because some questions will challenge both you and the folks you're engaging with. But trust me—the rewards? They're well worth it.

Feedback Loops: Learning from Responses

So, you're trying to get better at asking the right questions, right? Well, one crucial piece to the puzzle is paying close attention to the **responses**—both what's said and what's not. Yeah, I'm talking about those verbal cues and subtle nonverbal signals. Sometimes, a flicker of an eyebrow or a half-second pause speaks volumes.

I've found myself, more often than not, in situations where I had to really tune in and listen, not just to the words, but to the rhythm of the conversation. It's a bit like learning a new dance, where every move and gesture carries its own meaning. There was this time I asked a coworker how they felt about a project we were both involved in. Their mouth said "everything's fine," but their hesitant pause and averted gaze told a different story—one that flagged I needed to probe a bit deeper, with sensitivity.

Regularly asking for feedback about how effective your questions are can be, frankly, a game-changer. After speaking engagements or team meetings, I often ask colleagues or attendees how they found the Q&A segment. "Did my questions open the floor for meaningful dialogue? How can I improve?" This practice not only helps me refine my technique but also builds trust.

When it comes to **responding to feedback** and tinkering with your questioning style, the key is to stay adaptable. Imagine riding a bike—when you hit a rough patch, you don't just keep plowing ahead; you adjust your grip, maybe slow down, or change course slightly. It's the same with communication. Someone once told me, "Your first question is just the opening act. Be prepared to rewrite the script on the fly." It resonated with me, particularly because tweaking your approach shows respect and attentiveness towards the person you're engaging with.

"Your first question is just the opening act. Be prepared to rewrite the script on the fly."

Utilizing responses to **refine subsequent queries** is, in essence, getting feedback in real-time. For instance, if someone shares a personal anecdote in response to a general question, maybe the next step is to gently dig deeper into that narrative, offering a blend of empathy and curiosity. It tells the other person, "I'm listening, and I care about what you're sharing."

"It's the feedback from those we communicate with that sculpts our mastery over questions."

Learning from responses means you've got to have your radar up, all the time. Checks like,

- Did my question make them light up, or did it cause confusion?
- Was there a shift in energy?
- Did the conversation deepen, or did it hit a wall?

These are like bread crumbs on the path to mastering systemic questioning. Now, this isn't a call to overanalyze every interaction to the point of inaction. It's more about being alert and present—ready to pivot, adapt, and refine. Because let me tell you, there's no one-size-fits-all when it comes to communication. Each interaction is a unique blend of opportunities... if you're keen enough to spot them.

This learning loop—this back and forth—is at the heart of meaningful exchanges. It's about reflecting on your approach, promoting feedback (**boldly**, I might add), and seeing every conversation as a chance to evolve. After all, the magic lies in the connection, in finding just the right chord that resonates with someone else... and, sometimes, the most profound insights are hidden in the simplest of responses.

Challenges in Mastering Systemic Questions

I'll be honest, mastering **systemic questioning** is tough! Why? Well, aside from the fact it requires a great level of skill, there's also **overcoming hesitation** and fear related to asking difficult questions. Nobody wants to be the person making others uncomfortable, right? The thought alone can make you sweat bullets. Add to that, when you're dealing with really **delicate topics**, like personal issues or conflicts, you've gotta have the touch of an artist to know how to ask questions in a way that's, well, not going to make matters worse.

"To ask the right question is harder than to answer it."

One major pitfall is letting personal biases get in the way of framing questions. We've all got them, those sneaky little opinions and judgments that color our perception. Recognizing and setting these aside is key to **effective communication**. Why? Because your aim should be to encourage open dialogue, and, let's face it, if you're coming at it from a biased perspective, you're likely to hit a wall faster than you can say, "What did I say wrong?"

Another huge piece of the puzzle is **balancing questioning with active listening**. Ever had a conversation where it felt like the other person was just waiting for their turn to speak rather than actually listening? Yeah, not very productive. Actively listening means you're truly hearing what they're saying and adapting as the conversation flows, which can lead to more genuine and constructive discussions. It's like... when you're trying to find a common ground, listening is the foundation, and questioning is, let's say, the framing.

Everyone's been there, right? You're in a conversation, your mind buzzing with questions, yet fearing you might cross a line. The trick lies in asking yourself, "How would I feel being asked this?". Empathy, guides us here like a north star.

Now, biases - I'm not just reiterating because I love hearing my thoughts, but because it's that crucial. I caught myself once, prepping for a team meeting, and my draft questions... oh, they had my personal agenda scribbled all over them. Took me a second, but recognizing this, I scrapped them, started anew, keeping the **team's objective** in sight, not mine. Liberation, I tell you.

"Questions open the door to dialogue and discovery. Ask them."

So, how do you tackle these challenges? Practice, reflection, and a bit of creativity. Maybe even drafting questions before a sensitive meeting and reviewing them. Does this question invite dialogue? Does it acknowledge their perspective? Is it loaded with any of my personal biases? A subtle shift in wording can make a world of difference.

Seriously, think about trying the following exercise. Next time you're in a discussion, concentrate solely on forming questions based on what the other person says, pushing yourself to truly listen, and then witness the magic. Does the conversation flow better? Are the responses richer?

Couldn't tell you how many times I've seen eyes light up when they realize I'm actually listening, genuinely curious. It transforms conversations, leading to places neither party anticipated, uncovering ideas and solutions that were buried deep.

The takeaway? Mastering the craft of systemic questioning is no walk in the park. It's more like trekking a rewarding trail with its fair share of obstacles, from personal biases to the fear of asking tough questions, and stumbling blocks of effective listening versus just hearing. But, as you inch closer to overcoming these hurdles, you notice something incredible. Your conversations get richer, more genuine. Problems begin to untangle, because, well, you asked the right question at the right time, establishing that much-needed connection. Ah, the power of asking... isn't it something?

Stimulating a Lifetime Habit of Curious Inquiry

Ever notice, after a really good conversation, how you feel both excited and kinda smarter? That buzz is often down to someone having the nosy knack to ask the **right questions**. Not just any old questions, but the ones that dig deep, make you think, and maybe even see the world differently... even if just for a moment.

Continuous reflection on past questions and answers plays a huge role. It's like looking back at a conversation and thinking, "What made that so darn good?" Or, "Why did that question flop?" Reflection helps improve your question-asking game, trust me on this one. For instance, if you ever asked someone, "What really makes you *tick*?" and got nothing but a shrug, maybe next time try, "What's something you **love** that most people don't know about?" Aha, see? A little tweak can open up worlds.

Let's not forget the Gold Nuggets of learning—**observation and analysis** of those who've *mastered the art*. Ever listen to those podcasts where the host asks such mind-blowingly simple but deep questions and think, "How do they even come up with that?" I do, all the time. Watching and learning from them is like finding a treasure map to hidden conversational genius.

Practice. Practice. Practice. Did I mention **practice**? It's like, without trying out new piano sheets, how would you play Beethoven? Talk to different folks, about everything under the sun. Animals, politics, cookies, dreams. Flex those questioning muscles across **varied subjects** to keep 'em strong and adaptable. And, **solicit feedback**. I know, I know, feedback can sometimes sting a *little*, but it's pure **gold** for growth.

"Every question is a doorway to a new world."

Commitment to practicing your questioning is like signing up for a gym membership and actually going. Daily. You won't see the muscles pop overnight, but give it time, patience, and **consistent practice** will you see transformation!

Learning from **mentors and peers**, soaking up wisdom from literature can open new doors. Think of every observation, every feedback, every book as a puzzle piece. Gathering enough of these can help you see the big picture of what makes an impactful question.

*"The art of conversation lies not just in saying the right thing, but in asking the **necessary**."*

Welcoming challenges is part of the thrill. You'll find yourself in mazes at times—**challenging territory**; with persistence, creativity, and curiosity acting as your compass... you will find your way through.

Speaking of creativity, let's talk about **precision questioning**. This is about cutting to the heart of the issue without dancing around it. It's tricky, requires a mix of intuition and logic.

Paying attention to responses, both what is said and what's unsaid, becomes crucial. Those sighs, hesitations, the spark in the eye—each is a byte of information. Use it wisely to tailor your next question. **It's like fishing**, only you're fishing for thoughts, feelings, ideas, not trout.

Finally, when a question goes south, or you tread into sensitive territory—Address personal biases, and balance your inquiry with **genuine care** and **active listening**. It's not just about hurling questions; it's about weaving them into a **dialogue**, making it as smooth as satin.

Adopt a **lifetime habit of curious inquiry**, and watch as it transforms not just the conversations you have but, sneakily, the very fabric of your life. It's a bit like magic, only it's real, and it's all in the power of asking the **right questions**.

Practical Exercise

Alright, let's explore what we're doing. It's **all about mastering the craft of systemic questioning.** Now, don't let the title scare you off. Sure, it sounds all official and fancy, but at its core, it's quite simple. We are going to learn how to ask **smarter, more effective questions**. Questions that make people stop and think before they answer. And yeah, it's sort of like becoming a questioning ninja.

Step 1: First up, let's grab a notebook or open a fresh document on your computer. I prefer the old-school charm of writing things down with a pencil—kind of makes you feel like you're crafting something special, doesn't it? But hey, you do you.

Step 2: Think of a situation you're curious about in your own life. It could be anything from figuring out why your room is always so cluttered (guilty as charged here), to why you can't ever seem to get your homework done before 9 p.m. Got it? Great!

Step 3: Next, we're gonna jot down the *most obvious question* you could ask about your situation. For example, "Why is my room always a mess?" or "Why do I always do my homework so late?"

Step 4: Here's where the magic of systemic questioning comes into play. Start by taking your obvious question and breaking it down into smaller, *more specific questions*. Instead of asking why your room is a mess, you might ask, "What time of day do I tend to toss things around?" or "Which items never seem to have a proper place?" Is your mind buzzing with ideas yet?

Step 5: Now, add a **twist to your questioning.** Think about how someone else who is really good at solving this problem might approach it. Would they ask something different? Perhaps they'd focus on solutions, like, "What smart storage options haven't I explored yet?" or "What routine can I create to tackle my homework sooner in the evening?" It's all about shifting your perspective to discover new solutions.

Optional Side Quest: If you're feeling particularly adventurous, find a buddy to swap situations with and try to come up with systemic questions for each other's dilemmas. Sometimes, a fresh pair of eyes can spot things you missed.

Step 6: After you've got your robust list of innovative, sharp questions—pause. Take a moment to look over them. Which ones jump out at you as being particularly thought-provoking? Pick at least three of these juicy questions and make a plan to act on them.

Step 7: Put your plan into action! Remember, the goal here isn't to find immediate answers. Instead, it's about getting comfortable with asking deeper, more purposeful questions. Over the next week, keep this list of questions handy. And every time you tackle one, jot down any new insights or observations that come to mind.

Final Reflection: After a week of **mastering the art of systemic questioning**, reflect on how the exercise influenced your situation. Did you uncover any surprising truths? Did you make any changes that improved things, even a little? And were there times you got stuck and couldn't find an answer? If so, that's totally okay. Asking the right questions is an ongoing process, one that **requires patience, persistence, and a dash of creativity**.

So, there we go—a pretty straightforward exercise, right? I kinda think of it as training for your curiosity muscles. The stronger those get, the more natural it will become to dig beneath the surface of everyday problems. Keep practicing, and soon enough, you'll be the one everyone comes to when they need to cut through the noise and get to the heart of the matter. Who wouldn't want to be that hero?

Now go forth and question away. I'm rooting for you!

EXTRAS

logan.decodemymind.com/allbooks

Workbooks

Meditations

Affirmations

Audiobooks

DOWNLOAD

@loganmindpsychology

www.ingramcontent.com/pod-product-compliance
Lightning Source LLC
Chambersburg PA
CBHW071428210326
41597CB00020B/3699